# The First Heretic

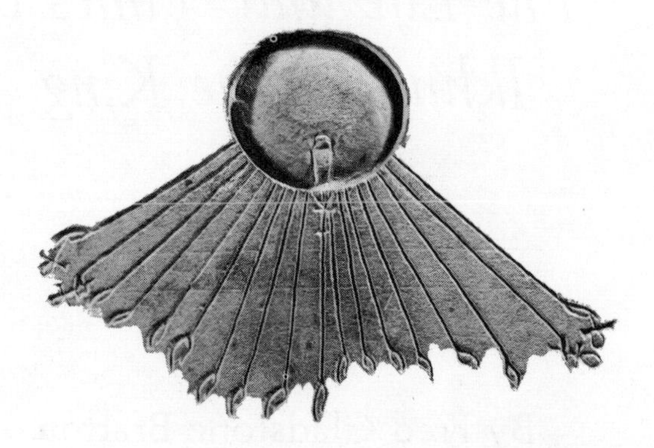

# *The Life and Times of Ikhnaton the King*

By Fred Gladstone Bratton

*Beacon Press Boston*

# THE FIRST HERETIC

*Published simultaneously in Canada by*
*S. J. Reginald Saunders and Co., Ltd., Toronto*

Library of Congress catalog card number: 61–13119

*Printed in the United States of America*

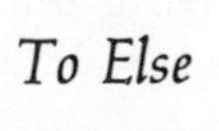

*To Else*

## Acknowledgments

I wish to thank the following publishers for permission to quote from the works cited:

Oxford University Press ("The Hymn to the Nile" reprinted from *A Comparative Study of the Literature of Egypt, Palestine, and Mesopotamia* by T. Eric Peet, published for the British Academy; copyright 1931).

University of Chicago Press (Silsileh and stele inscriptions reprinted from *Ancient Records of Egypt*, Vol. 2, by James H. Breasted; copyright 1906 by the University of Chicago).

Charles Scribner's Sons (Ikhnaton's "Hymn to the Sun" and selected sayings of Amen-em-ope reprinted from *The Dawn of Conscience* by James H. Breasted; copyright 1933 by James H. Breasted).

American Sunday-School Union (Letter of Ebed-Hepa reprinted from *Archaeology and the Bible*, 5th ed., by George A. Barton; copyright 1927 by American Sunday-School Union).

Princeton University Press (portions of letter of Rib-Addi reprinted from *Ancient Near Eastern Texts Relating to the Old Testament*, 2nd ed., edited by James B. Pritchard; copyright 1955).

*Facing title page:* Cast head of Ikhnaton from Tell el-Amarna. (Photograph by Walter Steinkopf, Berlin-Dahlem. Berlin Museum.)

# Foreword

A detached attitude, especially toward the remote and partially unknown, can bar from sight those many vistas glimpsed by the historian who approaches the task of reconstructing an era with sympathy, affection and imagination. In recording the life of Ikhnaton, I have eulogized him. The strength and warmth of his intellect require a similar warmth in its depiction; and neither the accuracy nor the equilibrium of scholarship are upset by controlled imagination and honest praise.

Though eulogy need not conflict with scholarship, it must conflict with theories of historical inevitability, which deny that a single great man can profoundly alter the course of events. I have written this book as a protest against such deterministic philosophies of history. Protest is needed, since at mid-century this de-emphasis of the individual and his influence has passed from historiography into our culture at large. Too much of our current literature and thought rejects the role of the hero in history, denies the importance of individual genius in social change, refuses to recognize superiority, and fears eccentricity and dissent. This determinism has its immediate historical origin in the debunking period of the 1920s. Debunking was then a salutary corrective in American biography, lowering the Victorian pedestal of the haloed hero and making possible an improved synthesis of fine journalistic style with critical scholarship in the biographical writing of the 1930s. But at mid-century, debunking has reappeared in the form of a systematic and dulling determinism, which threatens to sap the vitality from all serious biography of significant lives.

Historical fatalism has received increasingly influential support, while it has appeared in increasingly varied guises: Calvin's " theological determinism," Hegel's " world spirit," Marx's " inevitable dialectic," Tolstoi's " Things happen because they were bound to happen," Spengler's and later Toynbee's " cyclic theory of cultures," Sorokin's " irresistible socio-cultural currents " and A. L. Kroeber's " deep-seated, blind, and intricate forces that shape culture." The deterministic prevails over the purposive and the social prevails over the individual. The historical fatalists tell us that history is shaped by economic laws, social forces or divine will, and that these inexorable necessities go their way uninfluenced by individual geniuses. The hero is a particle caught in the drift of history, a mere by-product. What happened *had* to happen. Great men only *seem* to shape civilization, since progress — if it occurs at all — is its own creator. The great man is the "slave of history"; human will, choice and innovation are in reality nonexistent. So say the fatalists.

The fact is that social change, critical events and new movements in history are produced as much by the originality and power of great men as by blind social forces grinding along on their inevitable courses. Confucius, Michelangelo, Shakespeare, Spinoza, Newton, Beethoven and others like them achieved creative expressions which were far more than reflections of the times or by-products of irresistible social forces. The titans of history have not supplied needs of the moment; rather they have run counter to their times, generating forces that changed history. It is still true that every significant movement in history is " the lengthened shadow of a great man."

Men can and do determine their own destiny. Whether for good or for evil, individual genius has made civilization. Fatalism is not a philosophical and historical truth, but an escape from responsibility and possibility. Historical inevitability is an excuse for the denial of freedom. The rejection of the hero is an excuse for mediocrity. The churlish refusal to acknowledge excellence is a last refuge of the small man.

I am portraying Ikhnaton's life and thought not in order to worship a hero, but to recognize a hero. Ikhnaton took his stand against two thousand years of tradition, " drift of history " and preconditioning. He brought to life an idea new under the sun and lived by it. A hero of thought, he influenced world history more than most heroes of action. His life and teachings made him different in kind from all other kings and thinkers of the ancient world. The unique position of Ikhnaton was recognized by Emil Ludwig in his book, *The Nile*, when he wrote: " Only once in the history of Egypt was a revolution created from above (royalty, upper class); this was the achievement of Ikhnaton, the only Pharaoh whose life would be worth writing " — a judgment which provided ample justification for me — if such were needed — for writing this book.

Ikhnaton has become a controversial figure in recent historical researches and discussion; but all the facts are not yet in. Historians have attempted to strip him of his reputation for originality and genius by maintaining that his doctrines of universalism and monotheism were either not new or not revolutionary. They have called attention to his deformed appearance and possibly epileptic condition, and have claimed that he was unsophisticated in private life and naive in political life. Historians have called him " an unprincipled idealist," have insisted that " the trend of events would have been the same had Ikhnaton been but a sack of sawdust." One writer has called him " the mad Pharaoh, an inbred neurotic," whose doctrine of the sun cult was prompted by an obsessive fear of darkness. On the other hand, Ikhnaton's personality evokes unbridled admiration from other historians.

Whatever the true judgment of Ikhnaton's personality may be, his reign as pharaoh was the great divide in the history of Egypt, as well as in the history of the entire ancient world of the Middle East. The long story of Egyptian culture reached its most brilliant chapter in the Amarna Age. Cultural and political forces had built up a critical world situation, but the reaction to the world crisis was primarily the result of one man's personality. Ikhnaton shaped his times as much as Alexander or Caesar shaped theirs, but in another fashion. The first historically prominent individual to oppose the established order and the first thinker who both created and put into action original ideas, he was in fact the only prophetic voice in four thousand years of Egyptian history.

Whoever delves into the fathomless secrets of the land of the Nile, or is held by the fascination of its four millennia of history before the Christian era, cannot help but stand in awe before the great names of Egyptology, for they are great names and every researcher is in their debt: Mariette Bey, who assumed the directorship of the Egyptian Antiquities Service in the middle of the nineteenth century; W. Flinders Petrie, the grand old man of archaeology who founded scientific excavation in Egypt; James H. Breasted, whose works on Egypt are still the best authority in the English-speaking world for student and scholar alike; Adolf Erman, Breasted's teacher; Kurt H. Sethe, Erman's successor at the University of Berlin; George A. Reisner of Harvard, who excavated in Egypt for forty years; Gaston Maspero, director-general of the Egyptian Antiquities Service from 1881 to 1914; Arthur Weigall, inspector of antiquities for Upper Egypt under Maspero; Theodore M. Davis of Valley-of-the-Kings fame; Eduard Naville of Geneva, Switzerland; Dows Dunham and William Stevenson Smith of the Boston Museum of Fine Arts; E. A. W. Budge of the British Museum; Herbert E. Winlock of the Metropolitan Museum of Fine Arts in New York; John A. Wilson of the Oriental Institute of Chicago; Percy E. Newberry, W. B. Emery, S. R. K. Glanville, Pierre Lacau, Georges Legrain, Etienne Drioton, J. Capart, W. C. Hayes, Max Hirmer, H. Schäfer, W. Andrae, J. D. S. Pendlebury, Jean Leclant, Henri Frankfort, T. E. Peet, N. de G. Davies, James Baikie, Kurt Lange, James B. Pritchard, I. E. S. Edwards, A. H. Gardiner, Edward J. Quibell, F. G. Newton, H. W. Fairman, Georg Steindorff, Howard Carter, Lord Carnarvon, Ludwig Borchardt and John Garstang.

Particularly valuable in the preparation of this book were W. M. Flinders Petrie's *Tell el-Amarna;* James H. Breasted's *History of Egypt;* Ludwig Borchardt's reports on the German Amarna Expedition of 1912–1914; James Baikie's *The Amarna Age;* J. L. Smith's *Tombs, Temples, and Ancient Art;* Henri Frankfort's *The Mural Painting of el-Amarna,* and *Kingship and the Gods;* John A. Wilson's *The Burden of Egypt;* J. D. S. Pendlebury's *Tell el-Amarna; The City of Akhenaten,* Part I by T. Eric Peet and C. Leonard Woolley, Part II by H. Frankfort and J. D. S. Pendlebury; *The Intellectual Adventure of Ancient Man* by H. and H. A. Frankfort, J. A. Wilson, T. Jacobsen and W. A. Irwin; Kurt Lange-Max Hirmer's *Aegypten;* William Stevenson Smith's *The Art and Architecture of Ancient Egypt;* and N. de G. Davies' *The Rock Tombs of el Amarna.*

There are several accepted ways of spelling the name

used by Amenhotep IV after his inauguration of the Aton reform. I have used *Ikhnaton* rather than *Akhenaton* chiefly to avoid confusion on the part of the reader with Akhetaton, the name of the new capital which the king founded. Generally, I have used Amenhotep up to the time he changed his name to Ikhnaton. When referring to the new city in its historical setting, the name Akhetaton has been used; otherwise, the modern name of Tell el-Amarna. Apparent inconsistencies in spelling may occur here and there when another author is quoted or when, in the translation of an Egyptian text, the transliteration of the Egyptian name differs from mine.

I wish to thank Mr. Edward Darling, Mr. Karl Hill and Miss Mary Irving for their help in preparing the manuscript and Mr. Gobin Stair for his expert work on the illustrative material and format of the book.

FRED GLADSTONE BRATTON

*Springfield, Massachusetts*
*January 1961*

# Contents



# Illustrations

# I Files of a Foreign Office

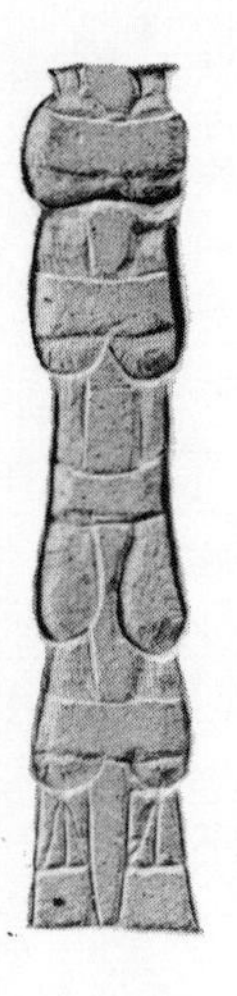

An overpowering feeling of permanence or changelessness soon strikes the observant visitor to Egypt. Coming usually from a country where the weather is unpredictable, where the sun is concealed by clouds as often as not, and where the temperature varies as much as 100 degrees, the new arrival is impressed by the uniformity here of the weather and the constancy of all things. So it was with the inhabitants of ancient Egypt, particularly as they contemplated the two natural phenomena — the sun and the river. The periodicity of the sun in its ride across the sky each day and the faithfulness of the Nile in its annual flood combined to give the Egyptian a sense of inevitability.

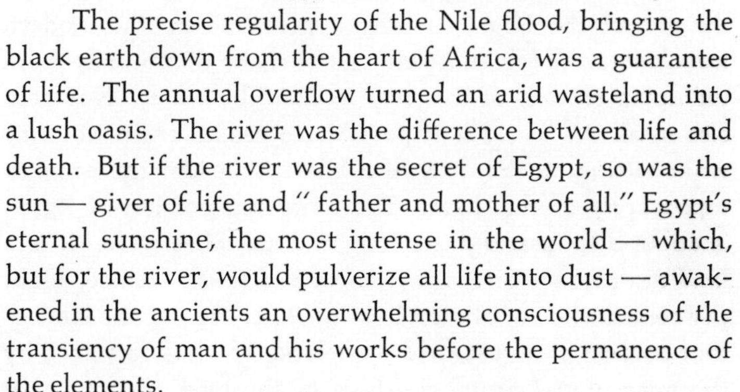

The precise regularity of the Nile flood, bringing the black earth down from the heart of Africa, was a guarantee of life. The annual overflow turned an arid wasteland into a lush oasis. The river was the difference between life and death. But if the river was the secret of Egypt, so was the sun — giver of life and " father and mother of all." Egypt's eternal sunshine, the most intense in the world — which, but for the river, would pulverize all life into dust — awakened in the ancients an overwhelming consciousness of the transiency of man and his works before the permanence of the elements.

Just as the sun followed its unchangeable course, bringing night and day, so the river rose and fell, bringing life to the soil. This regularity gave the Egyptians a profound awareness of security, a feeling further strengthened by their geographic isolation. Protected by the desert, sea and mountains, they did not share the anxieties of their neighbors in Palestine and Mesopotamia who were constantly in danger of invasion. The Egyptians had the added assurance that their land was ruled by a god-king who could not die. Thus, they came to believe that their civilization would never crumble.

The Egyptians were mistaken. Their civilization disintegrated, but not before it had achieved the longest and most productive culture in all history. With the exception of the brief period of Ikhnaton's reign, the theocratic society of Egypt remained inflexibly the same for almost three thousand years. No other civilization ever lasted so long. No other rulers ever wielded such absolute power as the pharaohs. No other people ever left so great a heritage of architecture, with the possible exception of the Greeks, whose Golden Age was born only after Egyptian culture had passed off the stage of world history.

The well-known phrase of Herodotus that " Egypt is the gift of the Nile " is fully appreciated by the modern traveler who is fortunate enough to make the journey from the upper reaches of the river to Cairo by water. Nowhere else in all the world is it possible to see an entire country while sitting on the deck of a boat. Consider the peculiar topography of this land. The inhabited portion of Egypt is about a thousand miles long and six miles wide. It is a land of only two directions: north and south. Ninety-eight per cent of the population lives on 3 per cent of the land — that portion of a vast, arid wasteland which is fertilized by the miraculous annual overflow of the Nile. Beyond that narrow strip on either side rise the high plateaus of the Libyan and Arabian deserts.

No other river offers such a diversity of environment or conjures up in the mind so many romantic scenes. Taking its source in Lake Victoria Nyanza, it travels north three thousand miles to the Mediterranean Sea. At Khartoum the White Nile is joined by the Blue Nile, and by the time the river reaches Luxor it has changed to brown as it gathers momentum and becomes wider. From the air the valley of the Nile is seen in three vivid colors: the reddish-yellow of the desert, spreading out on both sides to the horizon; the luxuriant green of the cultivated strips immediately flanking the river; and finally, depending on latitude, the brown or the blue of the river itself.

The landscape has survived as human fashions have not. Natives rushing to greet today's visitor at the river landing, crying "*Baksheesh,*" have no memories of ancient Egypt; the *dahabiyeh* has been replaced by the steamer; and even the crocodile has disappeared. But the sacred ibis still stand in black fields along the river banks and stalk gravely along the water's edge. The scene they survey has not changed: the timeless monuments of ruined cities along the banks of the river, the bellying canvas of the *feluccas* tacking before the wind, stately striding camels silhouetted against the late afternoon sky, water buffaloes turning the water wheels in the fields, *fellahin* laboriously working at the irrigation lifts along the muddy banks, women washing their clothes at the water's edge or filling their water pitchers which they place on their heads, the ever-changing coloration of the bluffs that enclose the Nile valley, the brilliant gold of the full noontide, the afternoon shadows and reflections, and finally the mysterious roseate afterglow that illumines the valley and then gives way suddenly to purple night.

At intervals along either side of the river, precipitous granite cliffs rise abruptly out of the water. But more often, one sees the mudbanks rising to the dense green of palms and other vegetation. Every inch of soil along the river is cultivated, even the little islands of silt which are made by the river when it is in flood, because the narrow strip of fertile earth suddenly gives way to arid dust plains which extend to the rocky wall of the desert plateau.

In its journey to the sea, the Nile plunges over a series of six rock formations called cataracts. Midway between the First and Second Cataracts — on the boundary between the Sudan and Egypt proper, at a point where the high plateau of the Libyan Desert forms the west bank of the river — stand four colossal statues, seventy feet high, carved out of the steep palisades which line the shore. They are the portrait figures of User-maat-Re, better known as Ramses II, and they form the facade of the temple of Abu Simbel. During his sixty-seven-year reign (1292–1225 B.C.), Ramses fathered one hundred sons, fought back his nation's attackers, and became Egypt's greatest builder. Well might Shelley write of him: "My name is Ozymandias, king of kings; Look on my works, ye Mighty, and despair," for he was the last and greatest warrior-king. He overcame the Hebrews, reducing them to bondage; he campaigned in Palestine and Syria to retain and extend the former empire; and he threw back the Hittites at Kadesh, in a battle fully depicted on the temple walls.

The temples of Ramses II are scattered throughout Egypt but the best preserved and most grandiose is Abu Simbel, gateway to Egypt and symbol of Pharaonic power. The complex consists of two temples, the smaller one of which was built by the king for his wife, Nefertari (not to be confused with Nefertiti, sister of Ikhnaton). Both temples are carved in the face of the sandstone escarpment immediately at the water's edge and are separated by a steep ravine down which the sand pours from the desert above.

*The Oriental Institute, The University of Chicago*

The Nile at Thebes is bordered on each side by the fertile plain and then the high desert.

The temple of Abu Simbel was once described by a French traveler as " the Cathedral of Notre Dame carved out of a single block of stone." However accurate that may be, its most impressive feature is the facade which is 108 feet high. All four of the colossi of the Ramses temple are portrait statues of the king, sculptured almost completely in the round against a facade background. These likenesses of the self-idolized pharaoh sit, hands on knees, serenely facing the east. The upper part of one of the figures lies broken at its feet. Greek mercenaries, almost a thousand years after the time of Ramses, carved their names and deeds in the legs of the king. Since the ancient Greek and Roman tourists knew nothing of the hieroglyph but could read Greek, these mercenaries became better known than the world-conquering Ramses! Beside the legs of the colossi stand eight statues, representing the king's mother, his wife Nefertari and six daughters, and between the legs are four additional statues, representing other daughters.

The interior comprises an enormous hall with three naves against the columns of which stand sixteen 30-foot statues of the king. On the walls of the temple are reliefs depicting the military campaigns of Ramses. One hall follows another to the chief sanctuary. When the morning sun bursts over the eastern cliffs and strikes the facade of the temple, its rays penetrate through the long pillared nave to the innermost sanctuary, bringing the silent figure of the sun-god to life.

For over three millenia, the four guardians of the temple have greeted the morning sun from the west bank of the Nile. But by 1970, Abu Simbel, along with some two hundred other monuments along the Nile, is destined to vanish forever. The newly proposed Assuan (Aswan) Dam will create a lake 300 miles long stretching from the First Cataract to the Third, half in Egypt and half in the Sudan, and will be two hundred feet higher than the maximum height of the Assuan lake. In 1960 UNESCO inaugurated a campaign to rescue the temple by constructing a protective earthwork around the site at a cost of approximately 50 million dollars.

Abu Simbel is indeed impressive. Only the river is more overpowering. Like " some great mighty thought threading a dream," its shores are a continuous museum of antiquities, recalling the glory of Pharaoh's Egypt. As we now make our way down the river, we pause briefly here and there to catch glimpses of that ancient glory.

At Assuan, the First Cataract, the water rushes through walls of granite and around the island of Elephantine. Lush with great palms and exotic plants, this onetime Jewish colony was the seat of the ancient Nubian ivory trade. On the granite cliff of Elephantine is a Nilometer, which tells us the height of the river inundation year after year for the last fourteen hundred years. One unforgettable experience at Assuan is the sight of the lovely columns of the Philae temples, bravely holding their heads above the waters, a dreamlike remnant of Ptolemaic and Roman days. Only in the summer, when the sluices of the great dam are opened, do the temples rise from their watery grave and reappear, their graceful columns reflected in the blue waters of the Nile. But when high water is reached in January, only the roofs of the temples break the surface of the water.

The island of Philae is a granite massif in the Nile measuring 500 by 150 yards. Before the erection of the first Assuan Dam (whose foundation was completed in 1902), it was a place of enchantment for those fortunate enough to reach such a distant spot. Palm trees, flowers and lush vegetation surround the magnificent temples. Built in the second century B.C. on the site of ancient sanctuaries, these temples were later embellished during the Roman occupa-

tion of Egypt. Today, in the summer months when the water is low, we can inspect the upper half of the buildings by rowboat. Dominating the island is the imposing Temple of Isis. We enter the giant pylons which flank the Great Court and then thread our way through the graceful papyrus capitals of the portico, stopping to admire the wall-reliefs which show the pharaoh making offerings to the gods. As we row away from the sacred isle of Isis, we reflect sadly that these treasures of Philae, along with those at Abu Simbel, may be lost forever, covered by two hundred feet of water.

Below Assuan the Nile widens as it deposits the silt carried for a thousand miles. Between the Second and the First Cataract the valley is narrow, usually not extending beyond the actual river bed; but here the fertile valley becomes broad, and green fields push out five miles or more to meet the yellow desert. Some forty miles from Assuan we pass the lovely temples of Kom Ombo, which were built at the same time as those of Philae. The Nile in flood has swept parts of them away but many perfect columns with their plant-leaf capitals remain. At Silsileh, a few miles farther, the Nile becomes a bare two hundred and fifty feet in width. Rushing through these narrows, the last in the journey of the river to the sea, we next come upon the Horus temple of Edfu, one of the most beautiful in Egypt. Built in the Ptolemaic period, twelve hundred years after Karnak, it was buried in the sand for centuries and thus was protected until Auguste Édouard Mariette, the French Egyptologist, dug it out in the 1870s. At the far end of the great court stands the regal statue of the falcon-god Horus.

At Luxor the Nile is wide and majestic and the mountains on either side are farther away, leaving a large fertile plain which once contained the proud city of Thebes. Our attention is first caught by the tall colonnades of the well-

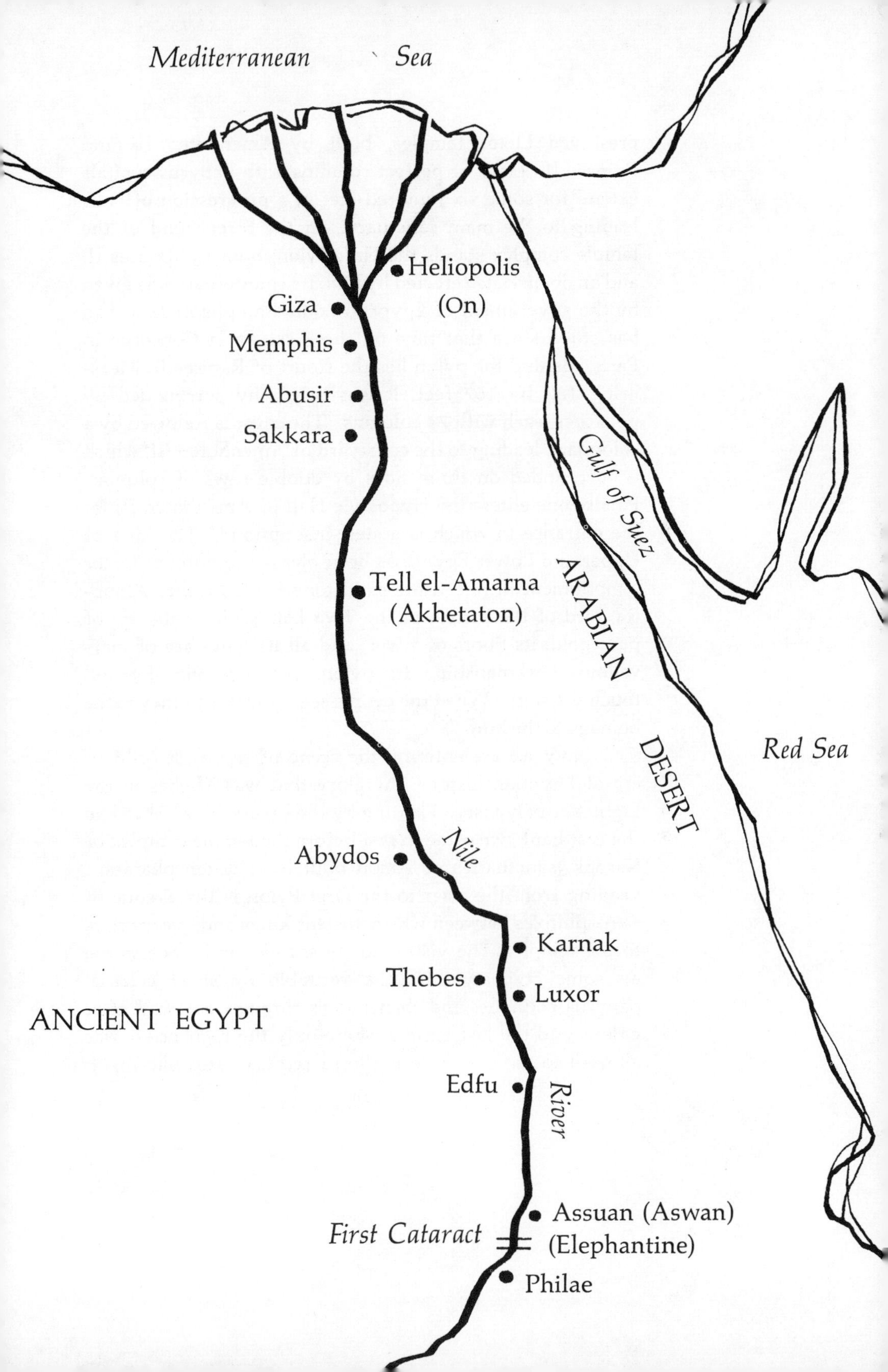
Mediterranean Sea
Heliopolis
(On)
Giza
Memphis
Abusir
Sakkara
Gulf of Suez
Tell el-Amarna
(Akhetaton)
ARABIAN
DESERT
Red Sea
Nile
Abydos
Karnak
Thebes
Luxor
ANCIENT EGYPT
Edfu
River
Assuan (Aswan)
(Elephantine)
First Cataract
Philae

preserved Luxor temples, built by Amenhotep III and Ramses II. Lines of perfect columns with papyrus capitals extend for some six hundred feet in a progression of halls leading to the main sanctuary. In the foreground of the temple complex stands the First Pylon, built by Ramses II, and an obelisk also erected by him. Its counterpart was given by the government of Egypt to Louis-Philippe in 1836 and has stood since that time on the Place de la Concorde in Paris. Behind the pylon lies the Court of Ramses II. Measuring 187 by 167 feet, it was originally surrounded by porticoes, each with 74 columns. The court is followed by a colonnade leading to the courtyard of Amenhotep III, which is surrounded on three sides by double rows of columns. Finally one enters the Hypostyle Hall of Amenhotep III, at the entrance to which is a stele inscription: "The king of Upper and Lower Egypt has been pleased to build at Luxor a monument in fine white sandstone for his father Amon-Ra, lord of the throne of the Two Lands. Its walls are of pure gold, its floors of silver, and all its gates are of marvellous workmanship. Its pylons reach to the sky and touch the stars. When the people see these things they make homage to the king."

Now we are entering the scene of the most brilliant era of Egyptian history, the glory that was Thebes in the Eighteenth Dynasty. Floating by the luxury hotels that line the east bank, we come to rest before the temple complex of Karnak, sanctuaries of Amon built by a dozen pharaohs. Leading from the river to the First Pylon is the avenue of ram-sphinxes between which ancient kings and queens rode to the temple. The visitor today shrinks as he enters the awesome Hypostyle Hall, a veritable forest of colossal papyrus columns, and then passes through gateway after gateway to the last temple where only the high priest was allowed to enter. There is the sacred lake still filled with water. There also are the two rose granite obelisks of Queen Hatshepsut, one lying on the ground and the other standing perfectly erect, as beautiful as it was the day it was placed there.

The complex of Karnak consisted of twenty temples, the largest columnar structure ever built. The temples were so constructed on a northwest-southeast axis that the setting sun on one day each year — the summer solstice — shot a single brilliant shaft of light from one end to the other, penetrating to the pitch black of the innermost sanctuary. At that instant, just before descending behind the Libyan hills, the glowing sun struck the series of 800-yard-aisles and threw its blood-red colors into the forbidden depths of the holy of holies. Then it was that the priests, with the accompaniment of resounding cymbals and trumpets, celebrated the glory that was Amon.

Across the river, and dominating the Theban Plain to the south, are the so-called Colossi of Memnon, giant sandstone statues of Amenhotep III, sole remnant of his mortuary temple. They stand at the edge of the fertile fields, and in the summer the Nile flood swirls about their feet. The awe-inspiring Colossi, like the Sphinx, should be approached at night when the ravages of time and the mutilation of man are erased and the imagination supplies the facial features and expression of these timeless sentinels of the temple. It is at night that they come alive. The Romans called them the Singing Colossi because — so they claimed — musical sounds came from these giants every morning at sunrise. This phenomenon may have been produced by the heat of the rising sun, which caused the stones to vibrate and send forth a mournful sound. But now they are silent. The only sound to be heard is the singing of the *fellahin* as they follow the buffalo around the irrigation wheel at the feet of the Colossi, who pay no more attention to these workers than they did to Hadrian, Juvenal or Strabo, or to the Greeks and Persians before them. They sit there, immobile, looking at the rising sun, as they did thirty-five hundred years ago, completely indifferent to the procession of pharaohs as dynasties came and went — symbol of changeless Egypt.

Nearby, at Deir el-Bahri, is the mortuary temple of the woman pharaoh, Hatshepsut. This is a Greek-like structure of simple lines, built in terraces interconnected by long ramps. It was the work of the colorful figure, Senmut, the queen's architect and lover.

Farther to the north lies the famed Valley of the Kings, resting place of sixty pharaohs. Next, at Dendera, we pass the ruins of the holy precincts of the goddess Hathor, an enclosure measuring almost a mile in length, which was built in the Greco-Roman period. Here the river runs westward for about fifty miles and then resumes its northerly course. We pass Assuit, where a miniature Assuan Dam provides water for the surrounding cotton fields throughout the year. Here the Nile " oasis " widens to a dozen miles and the land is a Garden of Eden.

Some fifty miles north of Assuit, on the right bank, is a site which we might easily pass without knowing it. There are no pylons, obelisks or colonnades; one sees only palm trees lining the bank, and here and there a cluster of mud-brick houses. As the boat approaches the landing stage, curious natives quickly gather, for the infrequent landings here are regarded as a festive occasion. We climb the bank to the palm grove and rest. Three or four miles to the east rises an escarpment of hills that form a semicircle and return to the river at the northern and southern ends, thus making a natural bay of land. Equidistant along the palm strip by the river are three Arab villages. Why stop at this desolate place — an anticlimax, to be sure, after the magnificent monuments of Abu Simbel, Philae, Luxor, Karnak and

Thebes? There is little activity now except for some women who are working in the fields beyond the palm trees. And only the scattered ruins of buildings a few feet high among the sand dunes greet the eye. These ruins are really the climax of our little journey down the Nile. They are the remains of a beautiful city which for a quarter of a century flourished as the capital of the Egyptian Empire and then vanished from the earth — Tell el-Amarna or Akhetaton.

It was here, in 1887, that an Egyptian peasant woman, digging in a field on the outskirts of one of these little villages, stumbled upon some clay tablets in the sand dunes. They contained strange markings. She sensed that they might have some value and finally persuaded a fellow-villager to buy them for the equivalent of an American half-dollar. They were subsequently taken to numerous dealers who in turn sold them to archaeological authorities in Paris and Cairo, but these experts regarded them as worthless. Some were taken to Luxor and sold to dealers, and others were lost or ground to pieces. Finally a number of the tablets were bought by the Berlin Museum and the British Museum, where they were recognized as genuine documents of the fourteenth century B.C. written in the Babylonian cuneiform language.

Altogether some three hundred and fifty tablets were recovered and translated. The question immediately arose: "What were cuneiform inscriptions doing in Egypt and where did they come from?" The answer was not hard to find. Those tablets contained top secret correspondence from the files of the Egyptian Foreign Office. They were, in fact, letters written to the king of Egypt by his viceroys in all parts of the empire, pleading for help against invaders and warning of the impending loss of vassal states. Those letters provided the key to our understanding of one of the most critical periods of antiquity. They revealed for the first time valuable information about Babylonia, Canaan, Assyria, Mittani, the Hittites and the Amorites; and they recorded the first mention of the attempted invasion of Palestine by the Hebrews, two centuries or more before Joshua.

For centuries the sands of the desert have held the secrets of many lost cities before giving them up to the spade. With the discovery of the Amarna Letters the attention of archaeologists was drawn to that site, and the successive excavations have resulted in the resurrection of Akhetaton, as it was called originally, a beautiful city with harbors, temples, palaces, groves and homes, whose existence was unknown for three millennia.

There is a peculiar fascination in the contemplation of Amarna, the place where the famous portrait bust of Nefertiti was found and where Tutankhamon began his reign. As if by magic there sprang up a royal city, at once the nerve center of a vast empire and the seat of an unbelievable religious experiment that destroyed this empire. A wilderness suddenly became a world metropolis inhabited by Babylonians, Hittites, Cretans, Mycenaeans and Jews. Here lived the royal family, the nobles, scribes, priests, artists, workmen and slaves. Then, like a desert mirage, Amarna suddenly disappeared and again became an uninhabited desert.

The Amarna Letters made a lost age come alive. This extensive royal correspondence exposed the political unrest, the intrigue in high places, the political anxieties of the rulers. The letters were a scoop on the greatest international crisis of ancient times. In addition, they tell the story of the religious revolution in Egypt which was at once her greatest hour and her downfall.

It is no exaggeration to say that the discovery of the royal letters and the excavations to which they led far out-

*Cairo Museum*

A letter sent to Ikhnaton by a Palestinian king. Cuneiform tablet from Tell el-Amarna.

weigh in ultimate importance the discovery of the tomb of Tutankhamon and even the Dead Sea Scrolls. The Amarna excavations unearthed the painted pavements; the beautifully decorated walls of the royal palace; the fabulous busts of the king, Queen Nefertiti and the princesses, the rock tombs and the fourteen stelae with their inscriptions. But, most important, the excavations gave evidence of the art and family life of the palace, the hymns and poems that disclosed the magnificent obsession for which a king risked and lost an empire, and finally the records of the life and character of Egypt's greatest pharaoh and one of the most extraordinary figures in the history of the world — Amenhotep IV, who called himself Ikhnaton.

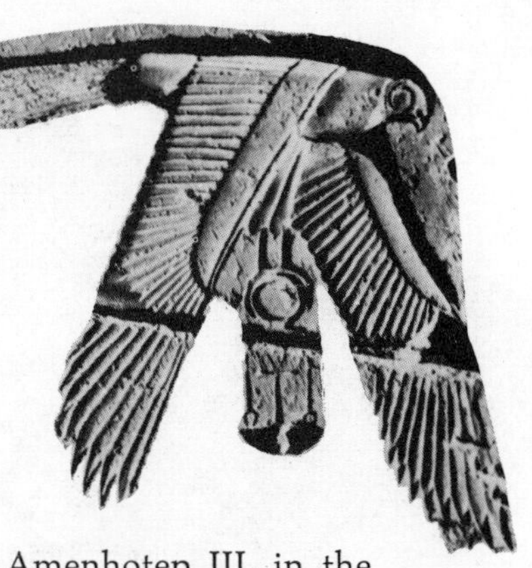

## II The Golden Age

It was in the great palace of Amenhotep III, in the twenty-fifth year of his reign (about 1385 B.C.), that the prince was born. Queen Tiy had at last given the ailing king an heir to the throne and there was great rejoicing in the royal household. The little prince was named Amenhotep after his father and in honor of Amon-Ra, but already forces were at work which would ultimately lead the future monarch to the rejection of Amon and to the transformation of the worship of Ra, the Heliopolitan god, into a new world religion. The tendency to oppose the ambitious priests of Amon and to encourage the worship of Aton had already been expressed among the members of the court, especially by the royal mother, Tiy.

The prince came from a line of sickly monarchs, so it was not surprising that even as a boy he showed congenital weaknesses. Both his skull and abdomen were malformed, and he may have been subject to epilepsy, although that is purely conjectural. His father must have looked with some apprehension toward the future, as it did not seem likely that his son would ever grow to manhood. This concern undoubtedly led to the decision that the boy be married and become a father as early as possible. Early marriages were common in ancient Egypt. Amenhotep III had married Tiy at the age of twelve.

*Photograph by Walter Steinkopf, Berlin-Dahlem.*
*Berlin Museum*

Portrait head in wood of Queen Tiy, mother of Ikhnaton and wife of Amenhotep III.

As a bride for the prince, Tushratta, king of Mitanni, proposed his young daughter. He was cognizant of his country's value to Egypt as a buffer state and knew the marriage would cement the union of the two countries. The proposal was favorably acted upon by Amenhotep, and the prince was married to Tadukhipa; but in the absence of any further information about her, it is thought that she must have died shortly after her arrival in Egypt.

Toward the end of his reign, the pleasure-loving Amenhotep III had been content to leave affairs of state to his chief wife, Tiy. The dominance of Tiy in the household during the early life of the prince made for a strong effeminate atmosphere, which was accentuated by the presence of at least two, if not more, Mitannian princesses, who were lesser wives of the king. Living in a palace occupied by a harem of several hundred foreign women was not calculated to educate the crown prince in the practical ways of men and the harsh world of facts. To say the least, this upbringing must have been an unrealistic and overly sheltered one; in fact, his devoted feminine tutors could only have catered to his fast-growing self-importance and self-sufficiency. Undoubtedly, while such a tutelage helped in the refinement of his religious thinking, it did not prepare him for an understanding of the emotions of men in the market place or for the strenuous life of a warrior-king.

The boy Amenhotep, as we have said, was noticeably deformed, thin and sickly. His abdomen and hips were disproportionately large, his jaws were long and his face was that of an ascetic. His features were delicate and his eyes were those of a visionary. He was quiet, thoughtful, affectionate. At an early age he liked to walk in the gardens and by the marshes, where he took delight in the singing of the birds and the fragrance of the flowers. But if his physique was weak, his intellect was not. His public and private life later testified to a wholesome and courageous mind. He was interested in things that did not belong to a king's world — theological and metaphysical matters. But he knew horses and could drive his chariot skillfully — daringly, in fact. But much of his time was spent worshipping in the small Aton temple that his father had built on the east bank, a dramatic foreshadowing of his future rebellion against the established religion.

Amenhotep IV came to the throne at the age of eleven (1375 B.C.). There can be no question that for the first few years the queen mother, Tiy, acted as regent. This entailed only a slight increase in the administrative responsibilities she had carried during the time her husband had been preoccupied with building monuments, hunting lions and acquiring a harem. Gradually the aging king had withdrawn completely from public life. Occasionally he had rowed about on his private lake, gone hunting or had been entertained by dancers and acrobats. It was Tiy who ran the government. Her importance in affairs of state is apparent in letters received from Tushratta of Mitanni, in which he assumes that the boy-king will confer with his mother regarding the contents.

> As to all the words of Nimmuria (Amenhotep III), thy father, which he wrote to me, Tiy, the Great Wife of Nimmuria, the Beloved, thy mother, she knows all about them. Inquire of Tiy, thy mother, about all the words of thy father which he spake to me. All the words together, which I discussed with your father, Tiy, thy mother knows them all; and no one else knows them.

The young king had inherited two advisers from his father's court: Ay, " the fan bearer on the right of the king, master of all the horses of his majesty, his truly beloved scribe," and Horemheb, the commander of the armies. Ay,

*Courtesy, Brooklyn Museum*

Ikhnaton and Nefertiti. Limestone model from Tell el-Amarna; with a hole for suspension at top.

who was also a priest, enjoyed an intimate association with Ikhnaton in administrative matters throughout his reign, a position of considerable prestige which must have continued afterward, for he actually occupied the throne for a brief time after the death of Tutankhamon, the son-in-law and successor to Ikhnaton.

But the most important personality in Amenhotep's life, his chief support and steadfast partner in all his thinking, was his sister, the princess Nefertiti, whom he married shortly after taking the throne. Although the face of Nefertiti is familiar to millions today because of her famous sculptured portraits, little or nothing is actually known about her. But all will agree that if her sculptor has faithfully reproduced her likeness, she must have been one of the most beautiful queens in all history. Some have suggested that she was of Mitannian origin, having been brought as a slave to the court of Amenhotep III and later renamed by the new king. This is hardly likely in view of the exact and detailed likeness of the sculptured heads of Amenhotep IV and his queen. It is further disproved by an inscription, found by Legrain, which refers to Nefertiti as the daughter of Tiy.

The new king and queen were young but it must be remembered that responsibilities came early in the ancient East; and under the wise supervision of Tiy, they rapidly became accustomed to their duties. The first few years of the reign were uneventful. Since there were no rebellions among the Asiatic provinces, military campaigns virtually ceased. Egypt was now content to hold her foreign possessions and exact tribute from them. Letters were received from the kings of Mitanni, Babylon and Hatti effusively lamenting the death of Amenhotep III and wishing the new king well. But all of these letters, and especially that of Shubbiluliuma, king of the Hittites, contained a curious

*Cairo Museum*

Unfinished head of Nefertiti. Found in 1933 in a house in Tell el-Amarna by the Egypt Exploration Society. In some respects this head parallels the fascinating beauty of the Berlin bust. Brown quartzite.

mixture of exaggerated grief and implied discontent, if not hostility, the grief being a necessary formality, and the hostility a not too veiled warning that trouble was brewing. The Hittite king wrote: " The messages which thy father during his lifetime was accustomed to send, why hast thou, my brother, in such a fashion withheld them? Now hast thou, my brother, ascended the throne of thy father; and as thy father and I were accustomed to request mutual presents, so now also will you and I be good friends mutually." Tushratta of Mitanni in another letter concluded his request for help with the statement that Egypt was a land of milk and honey, and Burraburiash of Babylon closed one of his letters by reminding the young king that his chief business should be to help finance his Babylonian colleague!

The young Amenhotep ascended the throne at a critical moment in Egypt's most brilliant era — the Eighteenth Dynasty. Egypt dominated the international scene. Art reached its greatest expression in freedom and naturalism. The temples and monuments outrivaled those of any other period. The kings, worshiped as gods, enjoyed untold power and prestige. Gold flowed into Thebes from Nubia and all Asiatic nations paid Egypt lavish tribute.

In order to appreciate the revolutionary character of Amenhotep's reign, it is necessary to understand his imperial heritage. Egyptian kings ruled like gods — with relentless power and yet with a certain beneficence. In fact, the Egyptians thought their rulers *were* gods, conceived by the union of a mortal mother with the god Ra, who assumed human form in order to cause the birth. Only by this divine birth could the pharaoh properly rule the land. When the king died, it was thought that he returned to the sun-god and was merged with him.

It was in the person of the king that the two parts of Egypt, which had always been separated topographically, were united. The king was called " Lord of the Two Lands " and wore a double crown. The dual title also implied that Horus and Seth, the gods of Lower and Upper Egypt, were merged in the kingship. A real national unity was created by the crown.

Not only was the king the son of Ra, he was also the incarnation of Horus when alive and was united with Osiris after death. Ra had given him a divine origin, while Horus gave him authority to rule all Egypt. One would think that a king possessing such qualities would be thoroughly isolated and inaccessible. In reality, the king was accessible to his advisors and court. Like the monarch of England today, he was slave to a rigid schedule of public functions, religious ceremonies and administrative duties. With the exception of such official appearances, however, the king maintained his isolation, thus reinforcing the aura of mysticism that surrounded the throne. The only king who mingled freely with his family and subjects was Ikhnaton.

As early as 4000 B.C., the office of kingship had been one of great prestige and power. In the First Dynasty, and perhaps before, the king was worshiped as a god by all subjects. His official title, in fact, was the " Good God," and the phrase " The One " — referring to the king — testifies to the observance of the ancient taboo against the direct use of the king's name. The government, represented by the monarch personally, was called " The Great House " or " Pero," the origin of the Hebrew term " Pharaoh."

The kingship — and ancient Egypt itself — cannot be understood without some grasp of two important concepts: the divinity of the pharaoh as son of Ra and the doctrine of *maat,* or truth. These two ideas had great cosmic significance for the Egyptians and might be said to constitute their metaphysics. Actually they are the two things that account for the long duration of Egyptian history. Just as the Sinai covenant provided the impetus for the Hebrew religion and served to hold the Hebrew people together in spite of all their vicissitudes, so this twofold tradition produced in the Egyptian consciousness the feeling of eternal existence, absolute certainty, cosmic order, and personal security. Because of the belief that the pharaoh was god and ruled in accordance with cosmic truth, the common man found his relation to the absolute or changeless order.

The dogma of the god-king meant that the pharaoh was not merely acting as an agent for god or as a mediator between god and the people, but *was* god eternally present on earth, presiding over the destiny of the land. Nor was the necessity of administrative officials and laws inconsistent with the divine rule of the king. The pharaoh *was* law; he was the state and whatever code existed came from him. All officials in the organization of the government came under him personally.

The eternal and unchangeable aspect of kingship was experienced in the artistic representation of royalty. Starting with the Fourth Dynasty, when the god-king concept became firmly fixed, relief sculpture and sculpture in the round assumed a rigid form which was never relinquished except in the Amarna period. All royal figures in sculpture, relief or painting were executed on a flat plane. This stiff, formalized art form was peculiar to Egypt. There is no evidence of foreign influences in its creation. Profile figures showed head and shoulders in a frontal position while the rest of the body was kept in profile. The rigidity and complete absence of movement or emotion lent an air of eternity to every statue. Such a static form succeeded perfectly in its aim — to depict eternal life. It showed the king in majestic repose, timeless, immobile, not unlike the later stereotyped figure of Buddha.

The static nature of the Egyptian culture, which was

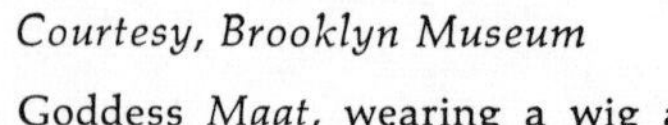

*Courtesy, Brooklyn Museum*

Goddess *Maat*, wearing a wig and high feather, symbol of "truth." Bronze.

the secret of its longevity as well as of its ultimate downfall, rests also on a second concept, *maat*. Depending on context, this word has a variety of nuances: order, justice, right, goodness, truth and harmony. Its principal meaning was a cosmic one and implied the harmony of the universe, the perfect order of creation as seen in the earth and sky and in the divine rule of the god-king. In this philosophical usage, *maat* was the definition of the ultimate reality, the source of cosmic order and the force that made and preserved stability. For an Egyptian living in an isolated unchanging environment, it was entirely logical to assume that there was an eternal mind behind creation which manifested itself constantly through the son of Ra. The close analogy of *maat* to the Chinese *Tao* is inescapable. *Tao,* as set forth in the *I Ching* (about 1000 B.C), refers to the Chinese philosophy of normality: keeping one's attitude and action in line with the situation at hand. To do the normal thing at any given time or season is the right path of behavior. To violate normality is an offense. In a larger sense *Tao* refers to the order and constancy of the universe, the way the world operates or " goes." *Tao,* the cosmic system, is an eternal process, the perfect way. It is the way of pure harmony and embraces all creation. When men cooperate with *Tao,* peace and righteousness prevail; but when men rebel against it, evil results.

The term *maat* refers also to that which is " just," " right " or " proper " in the sense that there was something proper and right in the cosmic order. It is the rightness of all things from the beginning. " Truth " is that which eternally is, the established order of life. But each man must cooperate and fit into that order so that the truth may be preserved. Thus *maat* can be translated " good," recalling the creation account in Genesis: " And God saw all that he had made and behold it was good."

The word *maat* was the Egyptian's conception of the ultimate reality; it was his basis of authority. It was his assurance of the eternal. It meant that all ephemeral phenomena are to be seen " *sub specie aeternitatis.*" All things that happened in the present life were but fragments of the eternal and could not change the plan of god. The evidence for this belief in an overruling providence was the god-king, the personification of *maat.* The king interpreted *maat* for the people through his administration of the land, appointment of officials and execution of laws. The vizier and other nobles were instructed to perform their duties in accordance with " right and just dealing " (*maat*). The lowliest workman should perform *maat* by taking care of his parents and obeying his master. In the administrative function, *maat* obviously contains an ethical meaning (although a utilitarian one) and refers in many recorded instances to just and moral human relations between employer and employee, between official and subordinate.

> If thou art a leader, commanding the affairs of the multitude, seek out for thyself every beneficial deed, until thy business be free from wrong. . . . If thou art one to whom a petition is made, be calm as thou listenest to what the petitioner has to say. . . . Long-lived is the man whose rule of conduct is right. Be not evil; patience is good. . . . Make thy memorial to last through the love of thee. . . . More acceptable is the character of one upright of heart than the [sacrifice of an] ox of the evil doer.

The Story of the Eloquent Peasant is an appropriate illustration of the use of *maat* in the ethical sense. Here *maat* was not used in the abstract, cosmic sense, but as synonymous with social justice, man's rights as man and the attitude of unselfishness. The story of the peasant, from the Twelfth Dynasty or earlier, sets forth clearly the responsibility of a steward to dispense justice impartially to all. In the course of his defense before the steward, the peasant illustrated the principle of *maat* in the case of the ferryman who carried a poor person across the stream without charge and the king who was like a shepherd always mindful of his flock. "Speak not falsehood," the peasant says to the steward, "for thou art great. Swerve not, for thou art uprightness (*maat*). . . . Destroy injustice; bring about every good thing. . . . Justice (*maat*) is for eternity. It descendeth with him that doeth it into the grave. His name is not effaced on earth, but he is remembered because of right. Such is the uprightness of the word of god."

Naturally the attendance upon the god-king brought into play an elaborate court etiquette and the employment of a host of lords, chamberlains and overseers. Tomb inscriptions give us some idea of the variety of court officials. Their duties often were highly specialized, as the following example indicates: "Overseer of the cosmetic box, working in the cosmetic art to the satisfaction of his Lord; overseer of the cosmetic pencil, sandal bearer of the king, taking care of the king's sandals to the satisfaction of his Lord."

The king had several wives in the royal harem, but his favorite wife was chosen as queen and it was customary for her eldest son to accede to the throne at the death of the king. Other sons from the wives of the harem were given vast estates and revenues or were awarded high positions in the government, many of which entailed great responsibility. Sometimes former friends or schoolmates of the king were made nobles and the king saw to their welfare while they were alive and, when they died, ordered magnificent tombs prepared for them.

Unlike many monarchs of later civilizations, the Egyptian king was not an unlettered despot who lived in luxury and idleness. More often than not he was an edu-

*Cairo Museum*

Bas-relief portrait of Ramose, vizier of Ikhnaton, and his wife. From his tomb in Thebes. Ramose was vizier to Ikhnaton at the beginning of the latter's reign and until the removal of the court from Thebes. (See following two pages.)

cated person, trained in the office of scribe or vizier or perhaps in the supervision of building operations, quarrying or mining. His daily routine consisted of such duties as consulting with the vizier, the chief architect, the military chief of staff and the secretary of the Foreign Office; receiving ambassadors, dictating letters to be sent to foreign envoys or to commanders on the borders of the empire and inspecting new buildings and projects.

Naturally there had to be some distribution of administrative responsibility in such a complex bureaucratic government. It was only by a system of delegated royal power that the country could be governed. The official who stood next to the king in authority was the vizier, who was given considerable power to administer in the light of his own judgment. He was instructed by the king to act according to legal precedent, to show no partiality in dispensing justice. He was told to " look upon him whom thou knowest like him thou does not know," upon the one who is " close to thy person like him who is distant from thy house." The vizier was held in fear but in great respect by all.

The office of vizier was introduced in the Fourth Dynasty. For a time it was held by a person of royal blood. Later, it was often held by a priest. There was a vizier for Upper Egypt and one for Lower Egypt. The vizier really was the head of the government and was responsible to the king for all the civil and military departments. He had representatives in every city who reported to him conditions throughout the country. All land transactions had to go through his office. He was the President's cabinet all rolled into one.

The government posts under the vizier were given to well-trained young men who had studied at court and had worked their way up through minor positions. It was possible for an ambitious and talented person to rise to a high position even though he had a peasant background. The head of the treasury held an important post directly under the vizier. He was responsible for all taxes and duties received from branch offices throughout the country. He also controlled foreign tributes and imports. Also under the vizier was the head of the department of agriculture. This branch of the government was obviously an important one, administering, as it did, all matters concerning animals, grain, sales of fields and agricultural taxes.

In a theocracy like Egypt, where ecclesiastical and civil matters were commingled, the high priest was an important official. The country was ruled by the god through the agency of his son, the king. In a sense, therefore, the king was a priest, for he served as mediary between the god and the people. The god revealed his will to the king who was accompanied by the high priest in the temple.

By the middle of the Eighteenth Dynasty, the priests of Thebes had made the rule of Amon-Ra more powerful than in any other period. As Queen Hatshepsut said regarding the period of the invasion of the Hyksos, Egypt had not been governed by the will of Amon. With her reign and that of her stepson, Thutmose III, the rule of the god became more pronounced and the high priest wielded as much influence as the vizier and the head of the military. In fact, the office of vizier and high priest of Karnak were combined under Hatshepsut, Amenhotep III and Amenhotep IV. Pharaoh was king, but the High Priest was the power behind the throne. The belief that it was the priests who held the keys to heaven insured their social and political prestige. Only the divinity of the king kept the priests from usurping the throne, as they had in Mesopotamia. The priests used their sacred profession to exploit and control the common people. They did this by selling all the objects

connected with burial rites, by taxing the people for the benefit of the temple and by presiding over the festivals. By these means, they became the richest land owners in Egypt.

The scribes formed a class almost as powerful as the priests. In a predominantly illiterate society, the literate, who had mastered the difficult art of writing hieroglyphs, acquired status. Good scribes were in great demand, and often rose to high positions in government.

The scribal school was attached to the court until the Eighteenth Dynasty. By then the education of scribes had become highly specialized, and each governmental department trained its own clerks after they had received the elementary instruction in the hieroglyph and the hieratic script, which was a cursive abbreviation of the pictograph system. Apparently, however, it was necessary to encourage the pupils, for we find numerous bits of propaganda exalting the scribal profession at the expense of other vocations. One of the " assigned readings " in a school for scribes ridiculed the life of the soldier:

> He [the soldier] rises in the morning only to receive castigation, and stands on the battle field every day. A lacerating blow is dealt his body, a double blow descends on his skull. A blow that knocks him head over heels is dealt his eyes, and a shattering blow falls on his nose. Be a scribe, that thy limbs may be sleek, and thy hands soft, that thou mayest go forth in white attire, honour done thee, and that the courtiers may salute thee. . . . Come, let me tell thee of the woes of the soldier; how that his masters are many, the general, the troop-commander, the major, the standard bearer, the lieutenant, the scribe, the captain of fifty, the platoon-commander. They go in and out of their offices in the palace. They say, " Produce the man that can work." He is awakened when but an hour hath gone, and driven about like a donkey. He worketh till the sun setteth,

*Archives Photographiques, Paris. Louvre*

Egyptian scribe holding a roll of papyrus. Fifth Dynasty (2500–2350 B.C.). Painted limestone. Found at Sakkarah.

bringing the darkness of night. He is hungry, his body is worn out, he is dead while yet alive. He receiveth his corn ration when he is released from duty, but it is uneatable when ground.

The scribe, according to one advertisement, is " freed from forced labor and protected from all work; he is released from hoeing with the hoe and need not carry a basket." He does not have to " ply the oar " and is his own master.

The scribe was an important cog in the wheels of business administration. Weighing grain, surveying fields, inspecting water, the work of tax returns, the departments of canals, fisheries, cemeteries and historical records — all depended on the office of the scribe. But for the scribe, the artist and the sculptor, we would know nothing of the civilization of Egypt.

While the priests and scribes were consolidating their skills and their political power, the pharaohs were increasing their military power and even turning from defense to aggressive designs. Ahmose, the founder of the Eighteenth Dynasty (1570 B.C.), inaugurated the most aggressive foreign policy yet known in Egypt. After driving out the Hyksos, who had dominated Egypt for more than a hundred years, and subjugating Nubia, Ahmose turned from liberation to consolidation. He set himself the task of restoring internal law and order. This was the beginning of a new and glorious phase of Egyptian history. Egypt had been jarred out of her isolationism and was now ready to take her place among the nations of the world. It became clear that unless she dominated the kingdoms to the north, they would dominate her. In the century between Ahmose and Thutmose III, Egypt became a world power with an empire that included Babylonia, Assyria, Palestine, Syria, Phoenicia, Cyprus, Hatti and Mitanni, all of which had to be held

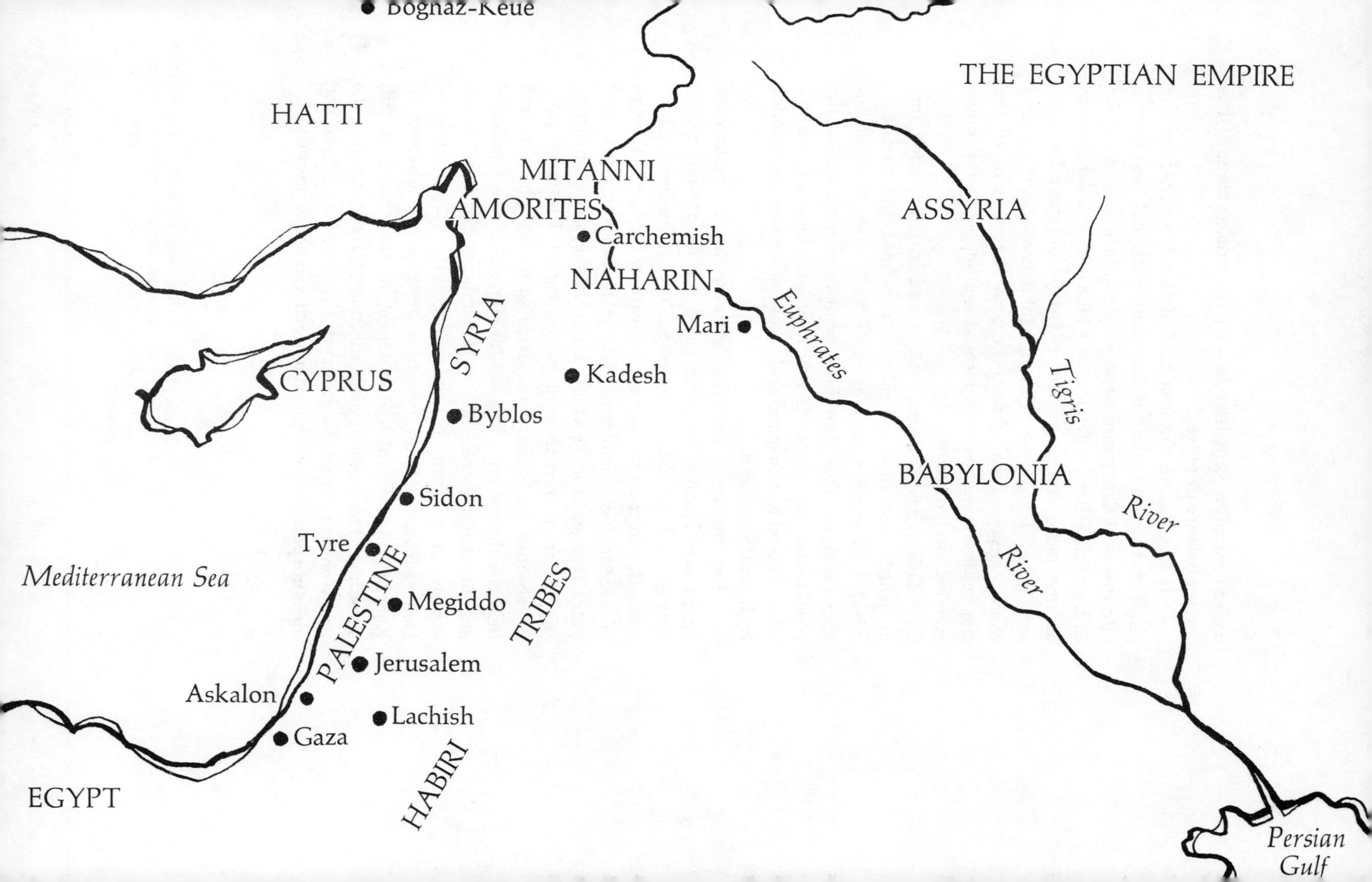
Boghaz-Keue
THE EGYPTIAN EMPIRE
HATTI
MITANNI
AMORITES
Carchemish
NAHARIN
ASSYRIA
Mari
Euphrates
CYPRUS
SYRIA
Kadesh
Tigris
Byblos
BABYLONIA
Sidon
River
Tyre
River
Mediterranean Sea
PALESTINE
Megiddo
TRIBES
Jerusalem
Askalon
Lachish
Gaza
EGYPT
HABIRI
Persian Gulf

under control or kept harmless by the preservation of the correct balance of power.

It was during the first half of the dynasty, from the reign of Ahmose to that of Amenhotep III, that Egypt came into the ascendancy internationally and held sway over the entire Middle East. Life along the Nile in the New Kingdom became more complex. The old days of quiet isolation were gone. The impact of foreign influences was felt everywhere: envoys from abroad were in residence in all the chief cities; slaves were imported from puppet states; kings married foreign wives.

This dynasty was an exciting and brilliant period, one in which women — either on or behind the throne — wielded as much power as their lords and, in some instances, more. The great ancestor of the female side of the royal house was Ahmose's wife and sister, Queen Nefertari, who outlived her husband and whose name was surrounded with great reverence.

But the most remarkable queen in the history of Egypt was Hatshepsut, who ruled for twenty-one years, first through the short reign of her invalid husband, Thutmose II, and then for seventeen years of the nominal reign of her nephew, Thutmose III. After serving for a few years as regent for the young king, Hatshepsut, with strong support from men in high places, thrust Thutmose completely into the background, declared herself pharaoh, and held the throne until her death. Her reign was a peaceful and prosperous one. She is remembered for her trading expedition to Punt, her magnificent funerary temple at Deir el-Bahri and her beautiful pink granite obelisks at Karnak, one of which, the tallest in the world, is still standing. The brilliant and ambitious Hatshepsut was the first woman to wear the crown of the Two Lands. She had absolute power and believed implicitly in her divine origin.

*Cairo Museum*

Basalt statue of Thutmose III (1481–1447 B.C.) from Karnak. For seventeen years his reign was usurped by his wife and half-sister, Hatshepsut, Egypt's greatest queen.

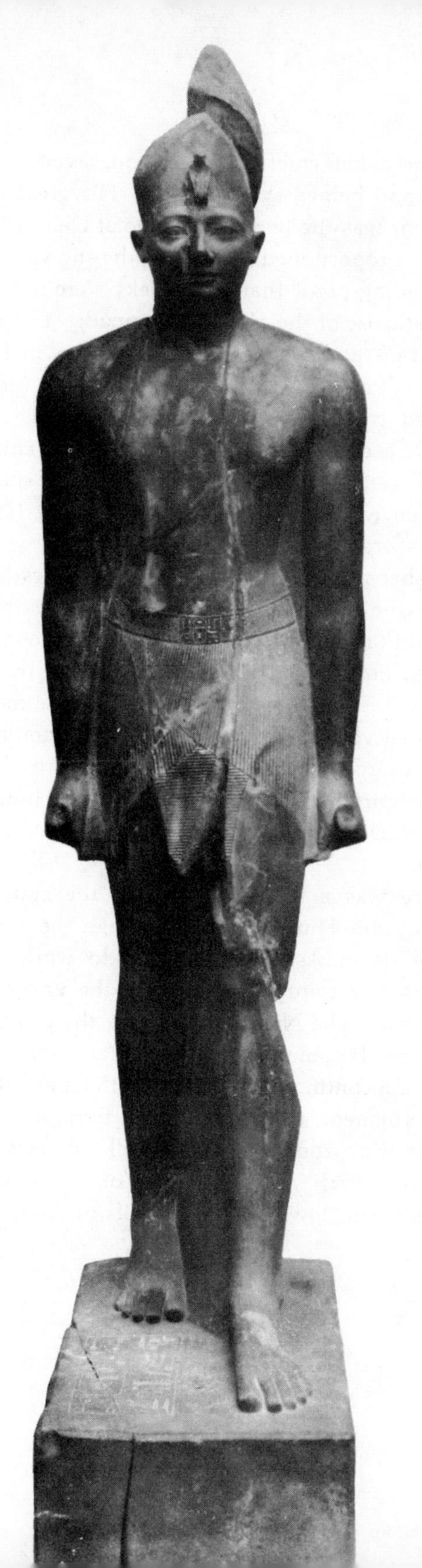

Senmut, her chief architect and favorite, shared all her plans and helped execute them. His greatest building achievement was the terraced temple at Deir el-Bahri. This beautifully proportioned building is the showpiece of Egypt and is standing proof that the Greeks were not the first to make artistic use of the exterior colonnade. The temple was carved out of the limestone cliffs in the bay of land on the western bank of the Nile at Thebes. Its three terraces were approached by long gentle ramps. The basic design is horizontal, accentuating the height of the cliffs. In the walls and columns of the temple are blank spaces — evidences even to the present-day tourist — of Hatshepsut's successor's wrathful resentment.

Hatshepsut had concentrated on domestic progress. But when she died, Thutmose III initiated extensive military expeditions abroad. After being held down for seventeen years, he released his pent-up energy by taking revenge upon the whole world. During his lifetime he waged seventeen successful campaigns. These triumphs — Gaza, Megiddo, Carchemish, Kadesh, Tunip — resulted in the first real empire in history and established Thutmose III as the first world conqueror, forerunner of Alexander and Napoleon.

There was a sharp contrast in the state policy of Hatshepsut and Thutmose III. Through the campaigns of Thutmose III in Asia, Egypt arose to world supremacy with a vast suzerainty extending to the upper reaches of Mesopotamia. The Nile delta became the center of world trade. Thebes became the most important city in the world, recipient of a continuous flow of wealth from a dozen provinces. Permanent troops occupied Syria and Palestine. Governors were appointed to rule all tributary states and collect taxes. Each year the armies of Thutmose returned to Thebes borne down with the spoils of Asia. The Egyptian treasuries were bursting with gold. After the king's capture of Megiddo, we are told, he brought back 924 chariots, 2,238 horses, 2,400 head of cattle, 200 suits of armor and vast quantities of gold and silver. The islands of the Mediterranean and the Aegean paid their yearly tribute. Conquest and power were in the air. Egypt was on top of the world.

After the death of Thutmose III, revolts broke out in Mitanni (part of the Hittite Kingdom), Naharin (the upper Euphrates region) and Lebanon. The new king, Amenhotep II, continued the aggressive policy of his predecessor and personally led his armies into these regions and subdued the rebellious forces, setting up a boundary tablet at his extreme advance in Mitanni. He returned to Thebes in triumph, bringing with him as prisoners hundreds of Syrian lords and ladies and much copper and gold. On one occasion he captured six Syrian kings and returned to Thebes with their bodies hanging face downwards from the prow of his ship. They were later sacrificed on the altar of Amon. His victories were so crushing that no further revolts were attempted in Asia during his reign. Shortly after his return to Thebes he marched southward and pushed back the Egyptian boundary in Nubia. That complete, he directed his energies to building temples and restoring monuments at Karnak and Thebes.

Amenhotep II died in 1420 B.C. and was succeeded by Thutmose IV. He, too, was forced to wage campaigns in Asia to hold the northern provinces. These were successful, and rebellion was further averted by his marriage to a Mitannian princess. He, like his father, quelled a revolt in Nubia and then returned to give his time to building projects in Karnak.

Thutmose IV was succeeded by Amenhotep III whose reign marks the turning point in the history of the empire.

At first all went well. Babylonia, Palestine, Assyria and Mitanni were still anxious to remain in the good graces of Egypt. The king of Babylonia wrote Amenhotep requesting gold on the grounds that his father had sent the Egyptian king a daughter in marriage. Another Amarna letter reveals that in the tenth year of his reign Amenhotep also received in marriage the daughter of Shuttarna, the king of Mitanni. Still later, Shuttarna's son, Tushratta, sent his daughter Tadukhipa, as the wife of Amenhotep IV. The royal correspondence of this period — so well preserved in the Amarna tablets — indicates the continued dependence of the Asiatic countries upon Egypt. The king of Syria writes: "My lord, here in this place I am thy servant. I am pursuing the way of my lord, and from my lord I do not depart. Since my fathers became thy servants this land has been my land, the city of Katna thy city, and I am my lord's."

Trade with Phoenicia, Syria, and the East reached an all-time high. The influence of Egyptian art and sculpture penetrated Mediterranean countries at this time. Thebes itself became a still more fabulous city, centuries later to be described by Homer as "Thebes of the hundred gates, where men's dwellings are rich, and rich the possessions, where heaps of precious ingots gleam." With unprecedented resources of wealth and labor, the king engaged in an extended building campaign. His temples and tombs were designed in a new and more beautiful style which was to serve as the chief source for Greek architecture and also for the later basilicas of Rome. At Karnak the king built a great pylon temple and at Luxor a papyrus temple which was never completed but which contains the finest columns in Egypt today. Across the river on the west bank he erected his mortuary temple with the two famous colossi, each seventy feet high and weighing seven hundred tons. The sculpture of this period reached an unexcelled refine-

ment and maturity. The museums of the world today contain many evidences of the magnificence of Amenhotep's reign. With each jubilee celebration, new and greater monuments were erected.

The splendor of the court of Amenhotep III can be appreciated from the descriptions on monuments and walls, and from the royal records. Heir to the security, wealth and prestige of Thutmose III, Amenhotep enjoyed his existence. The king built a beautiful palace on the western bank of the Nile opposite Luxor where he and his queen presided over a colorful court. The king's palace was a spacious, airy building made of brick and rare types of wood. The walls and ceilings were decorated with brilliant paintings of animal life and river scenes. Through the tall columns of the main hall one could look out upon the garden and beyond to the Theban hills. Nearby, surrounded by exotic flowers and trees from Asia, was the royal lake where the king and queen rode in their ebony and gold pleasure barge. This ornamental lake, over a mile long and a thousand feet wide, was built in the unbelievably short time of fifteen days. The significant fact about the lake, however, is not its size and swift construction but the name of the royal *dahabiyeh* which sailed its waters — "Aton Gleams." Little did the people realize as they reveled in the water festivals and admired the royal yacht that its name presaged the cataclysm that was soon to overwhelm their way of life, their gods and their empire.

During the reign of Amenhotep III, international trade flourished on an unprecedented scale. And, as we have said, with it came the ideological, artistic and cultural influences of every foreign country. The fact that the culture of Egypt reached its zenith at this time is probably due in some measure to this infiltration of foreign ideas. Thebes in the time of Amenhotep III was unrivaled in the ancient

world. The remains of the temples of Karnak, Luxor, and Deir el-Bahri are evidence enough of the architectural magnificence of the capital. The worship of Amon-Ra with its awesome temples, sacred barges on the Nile, hordes of priests and solemn processions was an impressive spectacle. The Theban priests, the most powerful priesthood the world has ever known, were an elite caste who made and destroyed kings and at one time owned one-third of the wealth of Egypt.

Amenhotep III had been married to Tiy in the second year of his reign. She was not of royal blood, but because of her husband's negligence and indifference, she gradually assumed control of the throne and was a formative influence in the early reign of her son, Amenhotep IV. Tiy was the daughter of two well-known figures in the court of Thebes, Yuaa, a priest, and his wife, Tuaa, a mistress of the robes or royal handmaid. Yuaa and Tuaa acted as advisers to the young royal pair and were highly respected at court. Both died about 1390 B.C. and were buried in the Valley of the Kings. Their elaborate tombs contained remarkable examples of the craftsmanship and art of the Eighteenth Dynasty. The mummy of Yuaa is probably better preserved than any other ever discovered.

As royal wife, Tiy received honors surpassing even those of Hatshepsut. Temples for her were erected, monuments to her were made and statues of her were sculptured. Her influence was felt not only in the new religious ideas of the day but in the new art, which reached its zenith at this time and during the reign of her son. Amenhotep III was concerned neither with religion nor politics, and in the latter part of his reign the power of the throne had passed almost completely into the hands of Queen Tiy. Her life was a full one, occupied with diplomatic and political problems, and with her artists, sculptors, and building projects.

*Photograph by Egyptian Expedition, The Metropolitan Museum of Art*

Bedroom of Amenhotep III, Malkata Palace, Thebes. Some of the ceiling, floor and wall paintings can be seen today.

The prosperity of the court exacted a certain price. It compelled a considerable generosity or, more properly, blackmail, in the form of a foreign aid program. The foreign correspondence of Amenhotep III and Amenhotep IV has a familiar ring. In practically every letter from Babylon, Assyria, Hatti and Mitanni there was the same threat: " Gold is the price of good will; we shall keep the peace if you send gold." " As for the neighboring kings, consider this," writes Burraburiash of Babylon, " if gold is forthcoming then between us will be brotherhood, friendship and happy relationship." Another Babylonian king promised to send daughters as wives for the king of Egypt if gold in great abundance was sent. Egypt had the gold; Babylon had the daughters. Foreign kings seemed to have many urgent projects that called for Egyptian subsidies: " Send me as much gold as I need for the completion of my new palace," writes one, and then continues, " surely I am as good as the king of Hanigalbat." Tushratta of Mitanni was probably the most naive and persistent of all these royal beggars: " So let my brother (Amenhotep) send me gold in great quantity beyond reckoning and let my brother send more gold than he sent to my father. For in my brother's land gold is as common as dust."

Some of the letters, however, were much more ominous, foreshadowing trouble in the provinces. The Hittites had invaded Mitanni and the Habiri were infiltrating Canaan. Reports came of the defection of certain Egyptian viceroys abroad and of the advance of the Hittites into Syria. If the king had listened to his advisers he would have known that all was not well and that the Hittites presented a great threat to Egyptian rule, but he had passed the time when he could rise to the occasion and take the field. In the thirty-sixth year of his reign, he died. His death left the Middle East unstable. Under Amenhotep III,

*Photograph, courtesy The Metropolitan Museum of Art*

Ikhnaton and Nefertiti standing with offerings to the sun-god Aton. A limestone relief from a balustrade on the temple ramp at Tell el-Amarna. The sun-disc has the uraeus (sacred asp) and *ankh* (hieroglyph for life). Now in Cairo Museum.

the New Kingdom had reached and also passed its peak development. Already there were ominous warnings of imperial decline, as reports of trouble came to Thebes from the various outposts of the Empire. The Hittites and the Syrians were in the ascendancy and threatened the dominance of Egypt in Asia. The other Asiatic nations were weak and depended on some stabilizing world power to hold them together. Clearly the future lay with Egypt. She was the only nation capable of mastering the world situation at a time when Assyrian, Hittite, Mitannian, Babylonian and Syrian interests conflicted. In this crisis Egypt needed its greatest king.

It is one of the ironies of history that at this time Egypt did receive her greatest king — but his greatness was not as a political or military genius. His only conquest was that of the mind; his only kingdom, that of the spirit. Amenhotep IV was a prophet, a philosopher-king. Egypt needed another Thutmose III to hold and extend the empire by military might, but instead it received the world's first pacifist, an idealistic dreamer. The situation demanded as never before a ruler skilled in the art of statesmanship and diplomacy. The new king brought to that situation the lofty and otherworldly ideals of a mystic, a king who had been counseled not by generals but by a woman, the queen mother. He was a sensitive soul who had no desire for martial glory and foreign conquest.

# III The Sun and the River

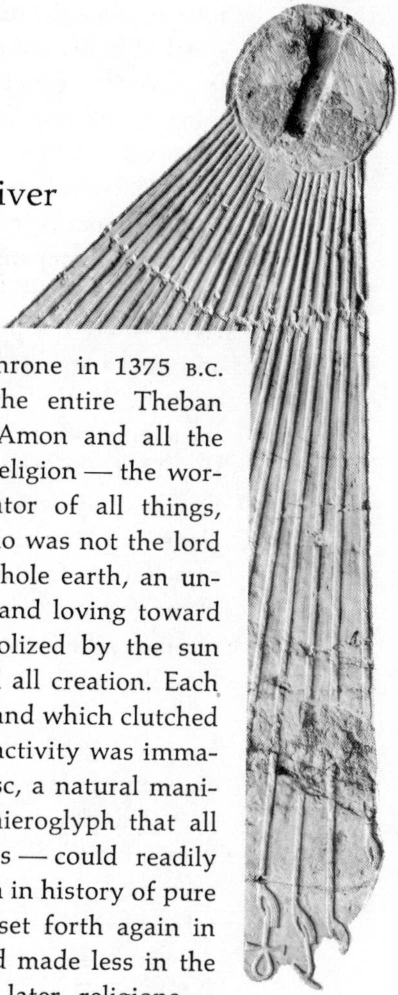

The young king who took the throne in 1375 B.C. parted with the military, overruled the entire Theban priesthood, discarded the worship of Amon and all the other gods of Egypt and set up a new religion — the worship of Aton, the universal god, creator of all things, "father and mother of us all," a god who was not the lord of any single land or race but of the whole earth, an unseen spiritual being, infinitely merciful and loving toward all his creatures. This god was symbolized by the sun disc, Aton, whose rays extended toward all creation. Each ray was pictured as ending in a human hand which clutched the symbol of life, showing that Aton's activity was immanent in all human affairs. The rayed disc, a natural manifestation of the divine energy, was a hieroglyph that all men — foreigners as well as Egyptians — could readily understand. This was the first expression in history of pure monotheism, a conception never to be set forth again in such a cosmic and universal form, a god made less in the image of man than the gods of the later religions — Judaism, Christianity and Islam — and completely devoid of their complicated and cruel theologies. By implementing this revolutionary ideal, the heretical king hastened his empire's end and his own tragic fate, since in his single-minded pursuit of his goal he brooked no interference and took no thought of adverse consequences, political or personal. But his failure earned him a reputation so unique in the records of civilizations that Breasted, the great Egyptologist, characterized him as "the first individual in history."

The new king found in his own coronation ceremonies further impetus for his rejection of the superstitious cult of Amon. Accompanied by Ay, the High Priest, Horemheb, Tiy and Nefertiti, he rode majestically in his chariot to the river, where the procession transferred to the royal ebony and gold barge for the trip to the east bank. Here they were met by the Amon priests who conducted them through the avenue of sphinxes to the Karnak temple of Amenhotep III. Then the prince was escorted to the entrance of the dark and mysterious Holy of Holies which he had to enter alone. In that dank, pitch-dark, forbidding chamber he came face to face with Amon and annointed first the statue of the god and then himself. Emerging from this impressive ceremony he was greeted by the priests as Pharaoh, god himself. But he knew he would still be the pawn and slave of the priests. It was a closed incident and he was only too happy to get back to the sunshine of the palace gardens and contemplate his new god Aton.

The development of Ikhnaton's thought must have been influenced strongly by Tiy, for the king could not have been more than fifteen years of age when he inaugurated his reform. Nefertiti and the priest Meryra, a convert to Atonism, encouraged the revolutionary direction of his thinking. He was now more insistent than ever that he was born of Ra, not Amon. But as long as he remained in Thebes he would have to go to the temple at Karnak to commune with the god Amon. He gradually became convinced that there was no truth in the Theban religion. He would create a new religion of light and beauty, a religion in which God would be worshiped as the cosmic force, the eternal creator, lord of the universe.

Prophetic genius is never wholly original and the solar faith of Amenhotep IV was not without some precedent. Theology frequently reflects social, political and economic developments. The isolation of cities and towns in early Egypt naturally resulted in a multitude of gods. As communication improved and national consciousness increased, there were fewer gods. But even in the earlier periods the solar religion was recognized in all parts of Egypt — a natural development, since the sun shone on all the land watered by the Nile. The sun-god Ra (Re) of Heliopolis, actually became a national deity.

As Egyptians came into a greater knowledge of the outside world, there was a natural expansion of their conception of deity. The real theological change came with the world conquest of Thutmose III. It is not surprising, therefore, that universalism in religion arose simultaneously with world rule, the shift from local and even national deities to the concept of universalism going hand in hand with world dominion. But this theological development which reached its consummation in the reforms of Amenhotep IV was a long and tortuous one, and it had its birth in the two natural phenomena that really define Egypt — the sun and the river.

Just as the Nile brings life and fertility in the summer and retreats in the death of winter, so the daily rising of the sun in the east brings renewed life to the soil and to man after the night of cold and darkness. In Egypt the sun is a reassuring fact. It is constant, relentless, subduing all; yet it is the giver of life and never fails. At Assuan the annual rainfall is zero, and throughout Upper Egypt it is little or nothing. In no other country does the sun shine with such an intensity and with such a constancy. The desert

absorbs the moisture; there is no fog or dampness. There is something inspiring about the daily reappearance of the sun with its healing power. In the sun's birth in the morning, its ride across the sky and its death in the evening, there was for the ancient Egyptian something more than meets the eye. The sun signified the secret of life and he bowed in reverence before it.

The conflict of the sun with the river produced in the minds of the early Egyptians a dualism which saw the sun as adversary as well as source of life. Its opponent, the river, appears as the savior of the life of Egypt by its annual flood which made fertile an otherwise arid land.

Yes, the sun and the river are Egypt. Indeed, it is not too much to say that the entire religious, political and cultural history of that country was determined by these two forces. The revolutionary movement of Ikhnaton can be understood only against the background of the two great traditional religions of Egypt and their identification with the sun and the river. It is not surprising that these two elements very early became associated with the two chief deities, Ra and Osiris. Ra, the sun-god, became the foremost deity and was combined with Amon, the powerful god of Thebes. Osiris was the god of vegetation and was symbolized by the fertilizing overflow of the Nile. Consequently life in the present as represented by the sun-god Ra and life in the future as symbolized by Osiris became the two dominant concerns of the ancient Egyptians. From prehistoric times the natural world made a profound impression upon these people. It was inevitable that the sunshine and vegetation by which they lived should be personified as gods. The sun-god and the verdure-god were gradually associated not only with the natural world but with human existence. Thus the insistent facts of life and death were blended in the Solar and Osirian faiths.

*British Museum, London*

Black marble nude figure of the sky-goddess, Nut, from Thebes. The daily course of the sun is represented in three places: at sunset it enters her mouth; at dawn it is born again from her genital organs; and pursues its course (between her legs). Twenty-sixth Dynasty (663-525 B.C.).

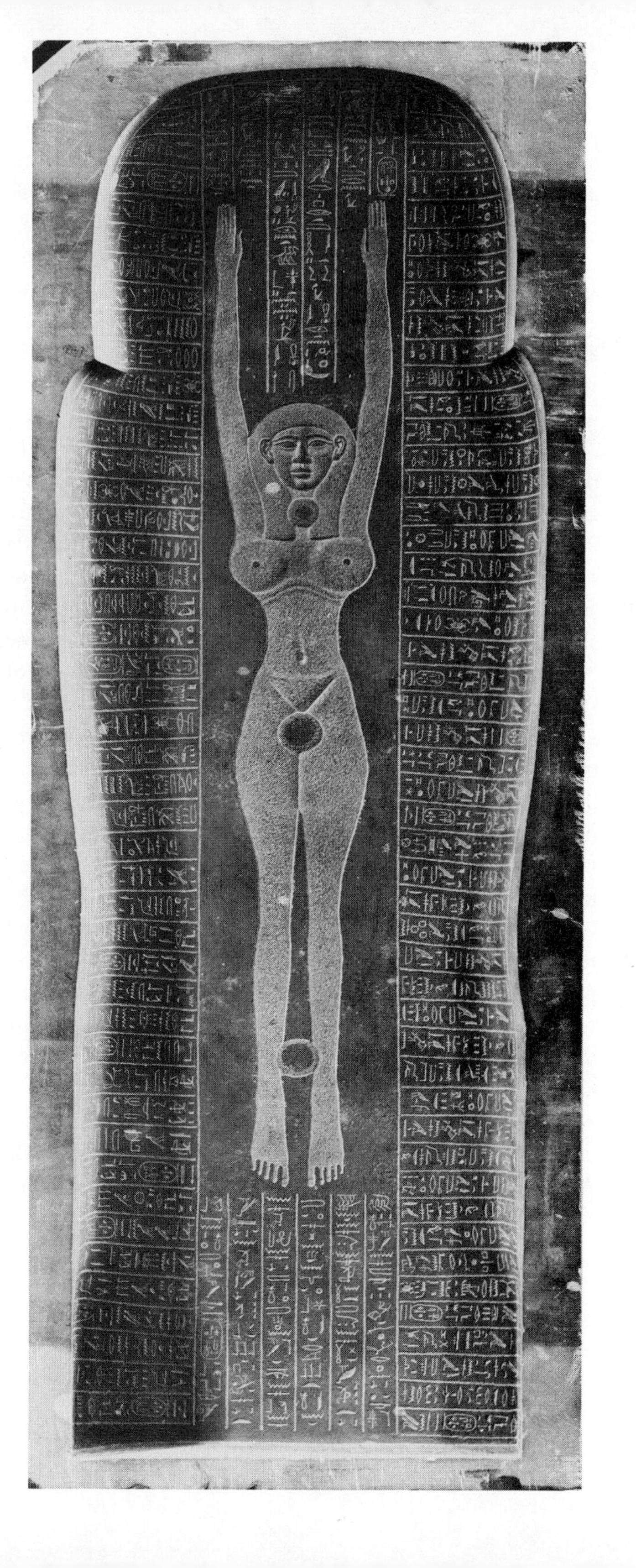

Like Alexander and Caesar before him, Napoleon paused to ask the Sphinx a question and then climbed the pyramid of Cheops. From this vantage point he exclaimed: " In Egypt, the Nile, the spirit of good, and the desert, the spirit of evil, are ever present." But the good overcomes the evil, for it is the Nile that holds the desert back. The black alluvial soil bordering the river on either side presents a striking contrast to the lifeless desert sand up to which the water flows in flood.

The Nile drew the people close together and united them in the common purpose of using the water wisely, gradually pushing back the encroaching desert. Only by uniting in an effort to control the flood, to actualize its gift of potential fertility, could the people of the Nile hope to survive. Clearly, the Nile was a formidable force in the shaping of Egyptian culture. The Nile compelled men to live by its laws. The Nile demanded a discipline and obedience that ultimately carried over into government and social life, producing a national character in which submissiveness, social cohesion and even a certain conservatism were dominant qualities. Every man who stood in the judgment hall of Osiris had to be able to say: " I have not sullied the waters of the Nile; I have not stopped its flow in the good time; I have dammed up no canal."

Even the architecture of the Egyptians bears witness to their dependence upon the life-giving vegetation of the Nile oasis. The papyrus and lotus columns of the temples were not merely functional pillars; they were the plants themselves, rising from the earth and touching the star-studded ceiling, dramatizing the life-process.

From the earliest times the land of the Nile was divided into two parts. Upper Egypt, from Memphis to Assuan, was distinguished by the narrow basin of the river between the high desert plateaus, while Lower Egypt was a broad, flat, delta region. Thus, Egypt was always known as the Two Lands. Politically, however, they were united as early as the First Dynasty (3200 B.C.). The union of the two was represented by the double crown of the pharaohs and by the early reliefs, depicting the two gods of the Nile tying the lotus of the south with the papyrus of the north, the traditional symbols of Upper and Lower Egypt.

Enclosed on east and west by the two high deserts, the Nile insured for Egypt an isolation and protection from invasion. To the north lay the Mediterranean and to the south, the cataracts. Altogether, Egypt was well guarded by natural features. In three thousand years of Egyptian history the country was occupied by foreign powers for only about three hundred years and the invading forces left little or no trace of their presence. To attempt to conquer a part of Egypt would be like cutting off a section of a worm which continues to live in spite of its loss.

It was the Nile that led priests to study the stars enabling them to calculate the time of the overflow. The measurement of the height of the inundation and the dimensions of reservoirs led to mathematics. The calendar, essentially, the same as ours today, was used before 4000 B.C. The administration of the problems of the river, combined with the concern for life after death that was associated with the flood and retreat of the Nile, necessitated written records. The beautiful hieroglyphic system of writing, originated as early as the First Dynasty, reveals the clarity and sense of organization possessed by the Egyptians. The material upon which they wrote was papyrus, a product of the Nile. The stalks were cut in strips, placed at right angles, and then pressed and polished to make an excellent and durable sheet for writing.

The records relating to the dead and the doctrine of

the future life are far more numerous and better preserved than those connected with social organization, business and family life. The reason for this difference is that the tombs and temples were in the desert and therefore survived, whereas the daily living took place in the green oasis by the river and written evidences of the common life of the Egyptians naturally perished in such a moist environment. Perhaps this accounts for the feeling that the Egyptians were more concerned with the life after death than with the present. To a certain extent they were, and that interest sprang from their dependence upon the river. A considerable portion of the literature of the Egyptians has to do with their adoration of the Nile, their great provider. Inevitably they came to worship its life-giving waters. " They tremble that behold the Nile in full flood," runs an early poem; " the fields laugh and the river-banks are overflowed; the visage of men is bright, and the heart of the gods rejoiceth." In the latter part of the Middle Kingdom the following hymn to the Nile was composed for the Theban festival of the inundation:

Praise to thee, O Nile, that issuest forth from the earth and comest to nourish the dwellers in Egypt. Secret of movement, a darkness in the day-time.

That waterest the meadows which Re hath created to nourish all cattle.

That givest drink to the desert places which are far from water; his dew it is that falleth from heaven.

Beloved of the Earth-God, controller of the Corn-God, that maketh every workshop of Ptah to flourish.

Lord of fish, that maketh the water fowl to go upstream, without a bird falling.

That maketh barley and createth wheat, that maketh the temples to keep festival.

If he is sluggish the nostrils are stopped up, and all men are brought low;

The offerings of the gods are diminished, and millions perish from among mankind.

When he arises earth rejoices and all men are glad; every jaw laughs and every tooth is uncovered.

Bringer of nourishment, plenteous of sustenance, creating all things good.

Lord of reverence, sweet of savour, appeasing evil.

Creating herbage for the cattle, causing sacrifice to be made to every god.

He is in the Underworld, in heaven, and upon earth,

Filling the barns and widening the granaries; giving to the poor.

Causing trees to grow according to the uttermost desire,

So that men go not in lack of them.

By far the most impressive literature of the river is that which has to do with Osiris in his functions as god of the Nile and the vast ritualistic formulae of the Book of the Dead. The earliest known references to Osiris connect him with vegetable life and its source, the river. "Thou, Osiris, art indeed the Nile, great on the fields at the beginning of the seasons, gods and men live by the moisture that is in thee." Water was the source of fertility, a life-giving agency in the soil.

Osiris represented the spirit of life in the waters, in the soil and in the grain. As such he symbolized the periodic death and rebirth of the earth, especially evident in the yearly rise and fall of the river. The Osiris myth tells us of his death at the hands of Set, his brother; of the weeping of Isis, his sister and wife; and of his resurrection. Horus, the son of Isis, avenged the death of Osiris, but in doing so lost an eye. The eye was healed by the god Thoth who spat upon the wound, a story which gained popularity later in Asia and which was probably the source of the legend about Jesus and the blind man. Horus sought his father to give him the eye he had lost. The eye of Horus became a sacred symbol of healing among Egyptians, evidenced by the countless " Horus Eyes " made of faience, glaze and precious stones, found in museums today. The eye of Horus also became the symbol of Egyptian medicine and is still used in a slightly modified form on doctors' prescriptions and in drug-stores.

To celebrate the resurrection of Osiris, an annual Passion Play was held at Abydos. Here the burial of the god was re-enacted and his death was mourned with great drama. Then the stones were removed from the tomb and the people shouted, "The Lord is risen!" In this rebirth of Osiris, the people saw their own triumph over death. The risen Osiris entered his realm as the king and judge of the dead. The influence of this drama upon the later Christian religion in its celebration of the Passion and resurrection of Jesus is unmistakable. There can be no doubt that the Syrian and Greek mysteries also influenced early Christians in their observance of the annual cycle of death and birth in nature and of the crucifixion and resurrection of their Savior.

The Book of the Dead contains three sections, the first of which is entitled " The Chapter on Entering the Hall of Truth." In this initial stage the deceased must testify to the god of Truth that he has consciously done no wrong. " I have not done evil in the place of truth. I have committed no sin against people. I did not do that which the god abominates. I allowed no one to hunger. I caused no one to weep. I did not murder. I caused no man misery. I did not commit adultery. I did not diminish the grain measure. I did not load the weight of the balances. I did not take milk from the mouth of a child." This testimony evinces an ethical awareness quite as pronounced as the Hebrew teaching of a thousand years later.

*University Museum, University of Pennsylvania*

The god Anubis leading deceased person toward the scales of judgment in the hall of Osiris. The heart is weighed against the feather (maat). If they balance each other, it is recorded by Thoth (illustration, page 60). Sheet of the Papyrus of Hunefer. New Kingdom (1550–1090 B.C.).

The second judgment scene is similar to the first and contains many of the same moral requirements: " I did not rob. I did not slay men. I did not steal. My fortune was not great but it was my own. I did not stir up fear or strife. I did not speak falsehood. I did not covet. I did not multiply words in speaking. I did not revile. I was not arrogant."

The third scene is that of the weighing of the heart of the deceased in the hall of Osiris. The heart of the person to be judged is weighed on a scale over against a feather, the symbol of righteousness and truth *(maat)*. The balances are operated by Anubis, the jackal-headed mortuary god. The verdict is recorded by the ibis-headed Thoth, scribe of the gods. Facing the balances are the goddesses of Destiny and Birth and behind them stands the person being judged. The verdict is witnessed by a jury of ten gods. If the verdict is favorable, Thoth announces: " Hear ye this word in truth. I have judged his heart. His soul stands as a witness concerning him; his character is righteous by the balances."

Having survived this test, the deceased is led by Horus to the judgment seat of Osiris, behind whom stands Isis. Horus announces that the deceased has a "righteous heart" and " has no sin in the sight of any god." Then the deceased is received into the kingdom of Osiris.

It is apparent that these judgment scenes, drawn over thirty-five hundred years ago, exhibit a distinct moral quality. This idea that each individual bears a definite moral responsibility exerted a profound influence upon the common people as the Osirian faith became the religion of the masses. A man had to prove his worthiness of eternal life by the way he lived on earth. Through the worship of Osiris, moral goodness became a paramount consideration.

The later teaching of Amenemope and Ptah Hotep reach a high level in ethical, if not in speculative, thought. To a great extent, the intellectual superiority of Egypt over

*University Museum, University of Pennsylvania*

The judgment in the hall of Osiris (illustration, page 59) is recorded by Thoth and the deceased is presented to Osiris by Horus. Sheet of the Papyrus of Hunefer.

other nations of the ancient Near East resulted from her wisdom literature, which wielded a considerable influence on the late books of the Old Testament.

As in all progressive cultures, life became more and more complex and tribal taboos and social customs proved to be an inadequate guide for behavior. Standards to govern human relations and private conduct became necessary. Thus the ethical sayings of the early Egyptian moralists gradually evolved, starting with the requirements for admission to the kingdom of Osiris. In the so-called negative confession, which the deceased person had to make before Osiris, there is an element of individualism not unlike that of the prophet Ezekiel. Each person stood alone before the god and was held responsible only for his own actions. His punishment, therefore, was self-imposed and his reward, self-earned.

The ethics of the immortality cult produced a prudential type of morality, with an emphasis on material prosperity, health, piety and worldly success. This particularly materialistic way of life later generated an Epicurean philosophy of pessimism and despair which finally gave way to an exaltation of the good life for its own sake, an ethic freed from both ecclesiastical compulsion and selfish ends. The good life was defined through human relationships and social values. Formerly, the criteria for virtue encouraged actions motivated by self-gain; now the criteria for virtue became contingent upon actions motivated by the welfare of another. Expediency gave way to principle and social concern took the place of individual piety.

The earliest author of moral maxims was Ptah Hotep, the Grand Vizier of King Userkaf of the Fifth Dynasty (*ca.* 2500 B.C.). His teaching took the form of instruction to his son in the life of common sense, practical wisdom and humility.

Be not proud because of thy learning. Take counsel with the unlearned as with the learned, for the limit of a craft is not fixed and there is no craftsman whose worth is perfect. . . . A listener is one whom the god loves. . . . The good fortune of a man is his understanding. . . . How worthy it is when a son hearkens to his father! How many mishaps befall him who hearkens not! As for the fool who hearkens not, there is none who has done anything for him. He regards wisdom as ignorance, and what is profitable as useless.

Much of Ptah Hotep's instruction concerns the kind of cunning that is prerequisite to obtaining worldly success. One should be circumspect, silent in the presence of a superior, obedient in all matters, careful not to offend and always humble, even when prosperous.

If thou hast become great after thou wast little, and hast gained possessions after thou wast formerly in want, be not unmindful of how it was with thee before. Be not boastful of thy wealth, which has come to thee as a gift of the god. . . . Be not avaricious in dividing. . . . Be not avaricious towards thy kin. Greater is the fame of the gentle than [that of] the harsh. . . . Repeat not a word of hearsay. . . . If thou art a strong man, establish the respect of thee by wisdom and by quietness of speech.

Another and greater wise man was Amenemope, who lived in the tenth century B.C. He substituted a theocratic principle for utilitarianism. Again, the moral maxims are directed to the wise man's son. The sayings of Amenemope are more reflective than those of Ptah Hotep and are based on a consciousness of God. After the prophet's admonitions to avoid corruption in business, to be honest in all dealings, to be prudent, temperate and gentle in spirit, he rises above the mere prudential type of morality and speaks of the life that is pleasing to God. He warns that earthly goods and worldly success are transitory.

The dependence of the Hebrew book of Proverbs upon the writings of Amenemope is clear from the following verses:

Incline thine ears to hear my sayings,
And apply thine heart to their comprehension.
For it is a profitable thing to put them in thy heart,
But woe to him who transgresses them.

Remove not the landmark on the boundary of the fields,

. . . . . . . . . . . . . . . . . . . . . . . . . . . . . . . . . . . .

Be not greedy for a cubit of land,
And trespass not on the boundary of the widow.

Weary not thyself to seek for more,
When thy need is [already] secure.
If riches be brought to thee by robbery,
They will not abide the night with thee.

Better is poverty in the hand of God,
Than riches in the storehouse.
Better are loaves when the heart is joyous,
Than riches in unhappiness.

Better is praise as one whom men love,
Than riches in the storehouse.
Eat not bread in the presence of a great man,
Nor offer thy mouth in his presence.
If thou sate thyself with unpermissible food,
It is but pleasure of thy spittle.
Look [only] upon the dish that is before thee,
And let it furnish thy need.

Consider for thyself these thirty chapters,
That they are satisfaction and instruction.

Unfortunately, the story of Osiris does not end on an ethical note. The priests undertook to sell inscribed sacred scarabs which gave magical potency to the wearer. The blessings of the hereafter could be guaranteed for a price.

*Photograph, courtesy The Metropolitan Museum of Art*

The well-preserved mummy of Seti I, whose career in death was as adventurous as that of his lifetime and whose tomb is the most elaborate to be seen in Egypt, is now in the Cairo Museum.

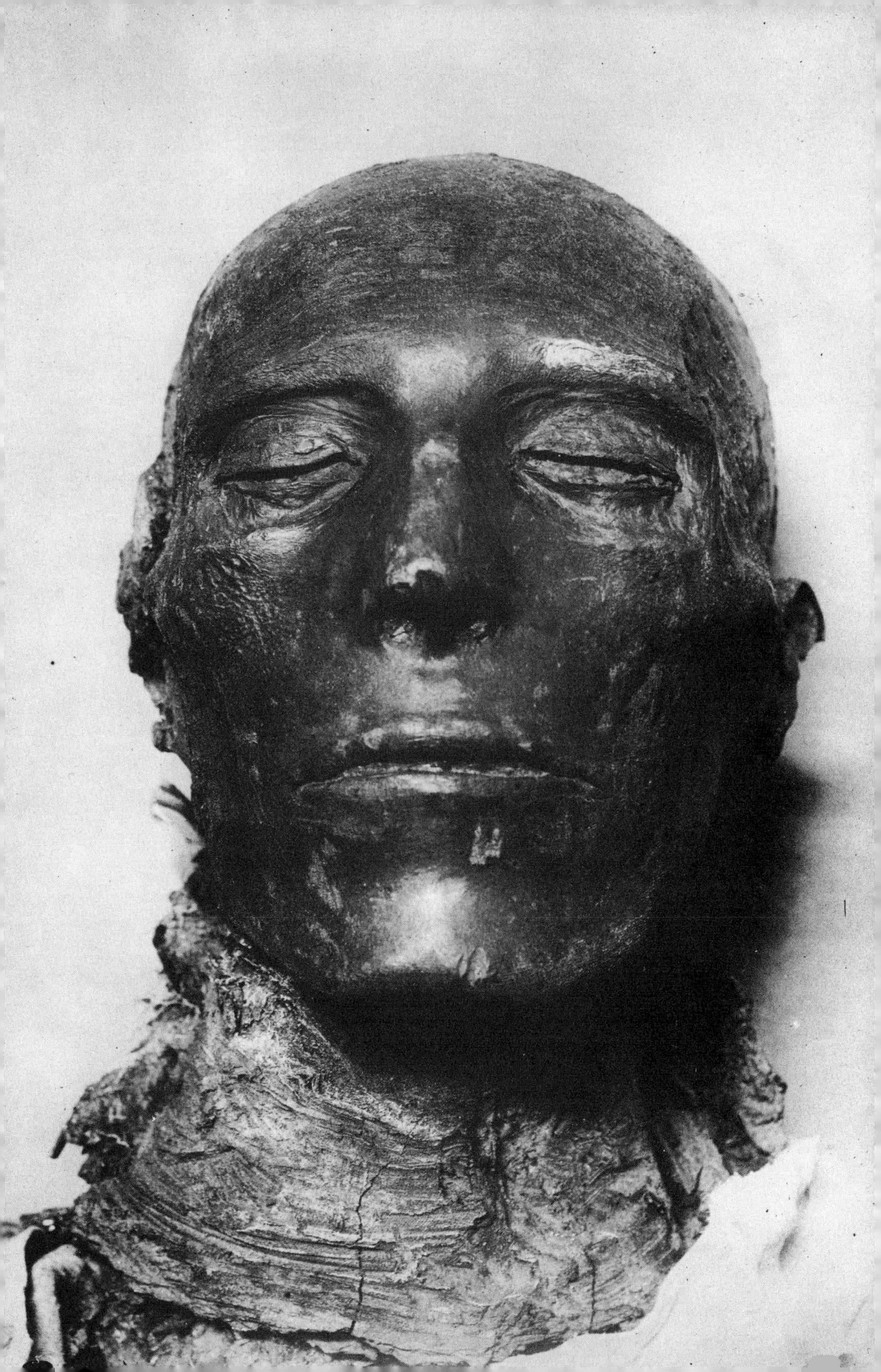

The priesthood and manufacturers profited by the sale of religious paraphernalia and the moral realm was invaded by superstition and commercialism. The Book of the Dead became a collection of prescribed formulae. The text of the Declaration of Innocence was written on papyri and sold to the people. The name of the deceased was simply inscribed in the proper place and his salvation became automatic. The papyrus rolls containing the mortuary spells were sometimes seventy-five feet long. So the Book of the Dead, which had been a force for moral responsibility, became an evil influence.

It remains for us to consider one further aspect of the Osirian cult, and that is the Egyptian concept of personality as related to death. The Egyptians represented the " spirit " and " soul " of a human being by the symbols " ka " and " ba." The " ka " was the vital principle or fundamental nature of a person. It was with him in life. It was also the guardian spirit which accompanied the deceased in the hereafter. Originally only kings were thought to have possessed a " ka," but later the idea was extended to the common people. Tomb paintings often show food offerings being placed in the tomb for the continued sustenance of the " ka."

The " ba," often pictured in tomb scenes, was represented as a bird with a human head and arms hovering over the mummy. It signified the breath or spirit of the dead person, and its presence served to impress the Egyptian with the idea that his personality was resurrected or restored to the body. The " ba " reanimated the body which then regained personality. A third term relating to death was " akh." This term specified a more spiritual or supernatural aspect of the individual. There is no sure way of defining these three ideas of the ancient Egyptians, but it is clear that their idea of the hereafter referred primarily to

*University Museum, University of Pennsylvania*

Section of the Book of the Dead written on papyrus in cursive or script hieroglyphic characters. The picture at the top shows deceased in a boat with sun-god and baboon. From Thebes. Eighteenth-Twentieth Dynasty (1570–1100 B.C.).

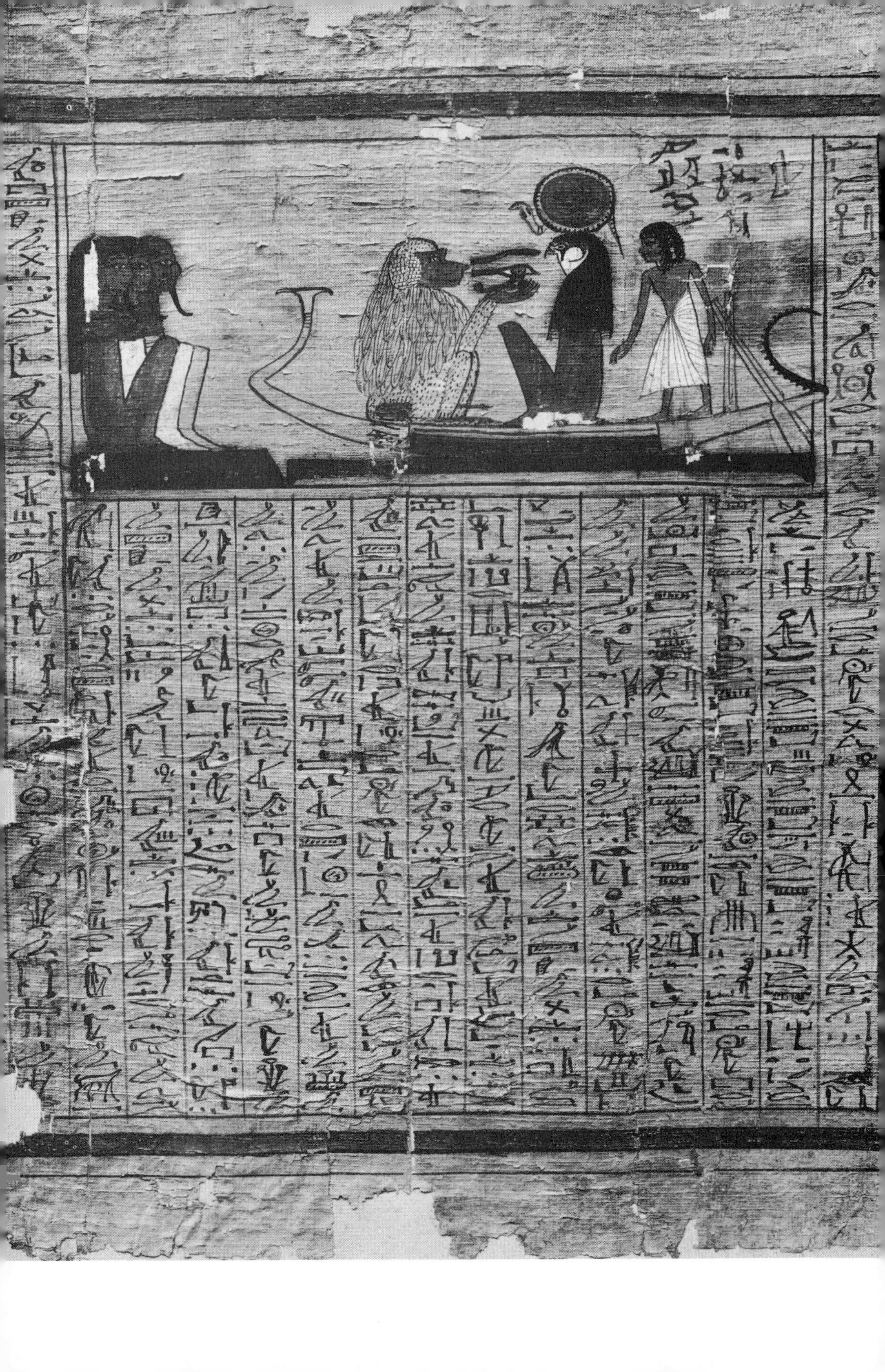

the body rather than to the soul; and their main goal was physical restoration by means of an external process. The body was resuscitated, so to speak, and thus became a spiritual entity.

The cult of Osiris was the religion of the common people. The worship of Ra, the sun-god, was more aristocratic since it had originally been the religion of kings. But because both religions had to do with the cycle of death and rebirth, the two were often compounded. Osiris was the god of resurrection, manifesting himself in the recurring overflow of the Nile and in the annual rebirth of the grain, whose dead seeds sprouted anew with the vital reviving power of the earth. Ra was the god of creation, the primal force, the father of kings and author of the cosmic order. His daily journey across the heavens from east to west signified his original appearance as the beginning of life. The regularity of the sun's course suggested to the Egyptians not only creatorship but justice and equity (*maat*).

The name Ra was often linked to the names of other deities to invest them with greater importance. In Heliopolis he was known as Ra-Atum, the god of creation. He was also known as Ra-Harakhti, the god of the eastern horizon; Sobek-Ra, the crocodile god; Montu-Ra, the falcon-god; and Amon-Ra, the god of Thebes.

In the cosmogony of Egypt, Ra was above all the creator-god. He was symbolized by the falcon and the scarab. The Book of the Dead speaks of Ra as self-created, existing before creation.

Hail to thee, sun disc of the day
Creator of all,
Who made their life;
Great falcon, feathered in many hues,
Who came into being to life himself;
Who came into being by himself without sire;

Eldest Horus who dwellest upon Nut;
Whom one acclaims when he shines forth
And likewise at his setting.

The creation occurred on a "primeval hill." The hillock arose out of the waters and was the source of all life. This idea probably referred to the first mound of mud that emerged when the Nile began to recede. No more logical location for the generation of life could possibly be conceived than this slimy mound rising from the fertilizing water and responding to the life-quickening blaze of the sun. Thus, we see again the combination of the sun and the river as the source of life, both spiritual and organic. Ra caused this birth and "ruled that which he had made" on the primeval hill.

The Book of the Dead with its description of the chaos, formless waste and total darkness before creation resembles the Hebrew account of creation in Genesis. Further parallels are seen in some of the Egyptian texts which say that man was created in the image of god, who also made the heavens and the earth, plants and animals and finally, man. The various elements of sky, earth, water, moisture and air were identified with other deities who shared in creation.

Ra was thought to have reigned as pharaoh in the remote past, and the kings were supposedly his descendants. In a sense, there was a rivalry between the divine king and Ra for absolute power and primacy in the minds of the people, but as son of Ra, the king could only be subservient to the god.

It is obvious that for the ancient Egyptians the most overwhelming and ever-present fact in life was the sun. Early pyramid texts testify to the localization of the sun-god in different forms. But with the union of Upper and Lower Egypt under King Menes (about 3200 B.C.), Ra the sun-god became " the sovereign of all gods," the god of nature and " the arbiter of human affairs."

The solar and Osirian faiths were related not only to life, but also to the insistent fact of death. The kings and nobles looked for a happy hereafter where they would live in the celestial kingdom of the sun-god. At Heliopolis (ancient *On*), where the official Egyptian religion was born in the Pyramid Age (2800–2250 B.C.), a temple cult developed with an organized priesthood devoted to the worship of the sun. In the Holy of Holies of the temple was a symbol called the *benben*, a pyramid-shaped stone representing the sun-god.

This stone fetish may provide the key to the religious significance of the pyramid itself. The king was buried under the sun-god symbol, which was placed in the center of the pyramid. The pyramid dominated the landscape for miles and its apex was the first object in all the land to catch the sun's rays each morning. Some scholars believe that the pyramid was simply an enlarged reproduction of the similarly shaped solar symbol in the temple. If this were the case, the pyramid must have been built to represent the rays of the sun slanting toward the earth. It is interesting to note that at times, especially in winter when late afternoon clouds form, if one stands by the Nile and looks toward the Giza pyramid complex, he can see the impressive spectacle of the sun's beams shooting downward through a cloud at the same angle as the sides of the pyramid.

It is also possible that the pyramids were phallic symbols, as some authorities have suggested, but it seems more plausible to connect the pyramidal form with the solar faith. In most ancient cultures the god was conceived as transcendent, and towers or temples were built to bring the worshiper nearer to the god. The ziggurat of Babylonia

*British Museum, London*

The sun-god as a falcon, rising from the desert with the sun-disc on his head. A painting from the Book of the Dead. (See also illustration, page 73.)

(the Biblical Tower of Babel), enclosed within the temple area, was one such high pyramidal building which the people ascended to be nearer heaven. Some of the early pyramid texts indicate that the kings saw the pyramid in this light. Several of these inscriptions speak of the pyramid as " a staircase to heaven being laid for the king." The Egyptian word for pyramid in its derivative sense is not clear, but there is reason to think that it refers to " a place of ascension."

The fact that the pyramid, associated symbolically with the sun, was also used as a burial place for the pharaohs is eloquent testimony to the profound influence of the solar faith in early Egypt. The capstone from the pyramid of Amenemhet III at Dashur (now in the Cairo Museum) illustrates this influence. On the side that had faced the east is pictured an ascending falcon with the sun-disc on his back. Under the sun-disc are the eyes of the king facing the rising sun. Under the falcon is an inscription: " The face of King Amenemhet III is opened that he may behold the Lord of the Horizon when he sails across the sky." The Book of the Dead frequently pictures the sun-god in the form of a falcon, with the sun-disc on his head, rising from the desert together with the deceased and his friends bowing in reverence before Ra.

Most of our information concerning the solar theology of early Egypt comes from the Pyramid Texts, the theme of which is the glorious destiny of the pharaohs in the realm above. For many centuries, both the prospect of being transported to the heaven of Ra and the preparation for the journey — including the elaborate process of mummification — were reserved for kings alone. Later, the rites connected with the doctrine of immortality were applied to all people and even animals.

The journey to the celestial hereafter was accom-

*British Museum, London*

The deceased lady and all the figures above her worship the sun-god, rising from the desert as a falcon. A painting from the Book of the Dead. (See also illustration, page 71.)

plished either by flight up the stairway of the sun's rays, or by sailing in a boat across the sky. A most striking illustration of the latter method is the funeral ship of King Khufu (Cheops), accidentally discovered in 1954 near the south face of the Great Pyramid. In the process of building a new road for tourists, workmen exposed a row of limestone blocks, each fifteen feet long and six feet thick, sealed with gypsum. This pavement turned out to be the roof of a long underground chamber containing the solar boat of the pharaoh which would waft the spirit of the king across the heavens. The craft, with its large steering oar at the stern, had lain undisturbed in its subterranean vault for forty-five hundred years. Kamal el Malakh, the Egyptian archaeologist in charge, found that except for the shrinkage of the wooden decks, the six-storied ship was completely intact. The hull, carved out of the natural rock, was one hundred twenty-five feet long and seventeen feet wide. This solar bark was probably one of several funerary ships required by Khufu as king of both Upper and Lower Egypt.

A year later Walter B. Emery, a British archaeologist, announced the discovery of another and older solar ship near the pyramids of Sakkarah. This ship comes from the First Dynasty, and although the wood was badly damaged, the boat still contained vessels for food and drink. These discoveries, as late and unexpected as they were, further confirm the very close relationship between the solar faith and the concept of the hereafter.

*The Oriental Institute, The University of Chicago*

Ramses III (1195–1164 B.C.) giving audience to the vizier and other officials. Hovering above him is the sun-god as a falcon, with outstretched wings, protecting the king. The phrase " under the shadow of thy wings " as a symbol of divine protection occurs four times in the Hebrew Psalms. A temple relief in Luxor.

*Cairo Museum*

Capstone from the pyramid of Amenemhet III (1849–1801 B.C.). This beautiful block of polished black granite was found lying at the base of the king's pyramid at Dashur. On the side which had faced the east is the winged sun-disc, surmounting the king's eyes which faced the rising sun so that he could behold the sun as it rose and started on its daily journey.

# IV Aton Is Satisfied

In some respects the Aton faith of Amenhotep IV was not a radical departure from tradition. As we have seen in the preceding chapter, the sun-god had always been the most important deity in the Egyptian pantheon, and the solar theme, representing the sun as the source of life itself, had always been at the heart of the Egyptian religion.

From pre-dynastic days sun worship had its national center in Heliopolis. The Heliopolitan cult of Ra, with its college of priests, exercised a significent influence on ritual, worship and religious thought throughout the early history of Egypt. This influence was so great that from the Fifth Dynasty on, every king of Egypt bore the title " Son of Ra." Some of the early literature ascribes to Ra a pronounced ethical quality not found in the later Atonism, although the absence from the Amarna inscriptions of any reference to this does not necessarily mean that there was no idea of righteousness at all in the Aton faith. In the Middle Kingdom (2134–1786 B.C.) the Theban Amon was identified with the sun-god and called Amon-Ra. Amon had been the god of Thebes, but when that city became the capital of Egypt he assumed a national importance. The goddess Mut (mother) was the consort of Amon and their son was Khonsu, the god of the moon.

It is at this point that an Asiatic influence may have been felt in the promotion and universalization of the solar faith. The wife of Thutmose IV, as previously mentioned, was a Mitannian princess, a worshiper of the Aryan sun-gods which resembled the Heliopolitan Ra, and it is possible that she had much to do with the shaping of the new solar religion. But this is only conjectural, and if there were foreign influences they merely served to augment a growth that was firmly rooted in Egyptian soil. It is possible, however, that this Asiatic connection produced a more syncretistic type of religion, ultimately leading to some dissatisfaction with the state religion of Amon.

There is no doubt that the universalization of the sun-god received considerable impetus during the reign of Amenhotep III. This is borne out by the description on the stelae of the king's architects, Hori and Suti, where the sun-god is described as holding sway over all lands and peoples. Ra was god, not of Egypt alone, but of all the earth. In a hymn of this period Amon is referred to as " Aton of the day, creator of mortals and maker of life." It is significant also that the royal barge used by Amenhotep III and his wife, Tiy, in their water festival was called " Aton Gleams," and that the royal title of the times contained the phrase " Heat which is in Aton ".

The reign of Amenhotep III displays a growing tendency toward theological speculation and a corresponding growth of indifference to Amonism, indicating, perhaps, that Syrian theology was beginning to exert a fairly vigorous influence. But because of the merging of Amon and Ra, the priests did not oppose sun worship as much as one might suspect. There must have been some mild attempt in the court to undermine the power of the Amon priesthood, to divorce Amon worship from sun worship and to introduce the name of Aton as the pure embodiment of the solar faith. This last effort freed sun-worship from any connection with Amon.

*Courtesy The Metropolitan Museum of Art, Gift of Edward S. Harkness, 1926*

A gold statuette of the god Amon, wearing a high crown the plumes of which have been broken. He carries a curved sword in his right hand and an *ankh* sign in his left.

At this time the more progressive members of the court and nobility were beginning to chafe under the tyranny of a priesthood which would not tolerate criticism or free thought. The growing power and wealth of the priests constituted a serious threat to the prestige of the throne. By the Eighteenth Dynasty the priesthood of Amon-Ra had become so powerful and wealthy that it virtually controlled the throne. The highest priest of Amon was the royal vizier; thus the highest ecclesiastical office was combined with the highest political office.

It appears, therefore, that as we come to the accession of Amenhotep IV (1375 B.C.) there is good reason for thinking that in establishing the religion of Aton he did not effect a complete break with the past, but in fact built upon it. That his theism was more universal, more monotheistic and more thoroughgoing than any previous belief is demonstrated by the tremendous animosity he provoked among members of the Theban priesthood. The genius of his reform lay in his conviction that the sun-god was not only the god of the whole world; he was the *only* god.

Early in his reign, Amenhotep IV probably realized that the original god of Egypt was Ra of Heliopolis and that Amon was really only a newcomer. He must have contemplated the fact that as pharaoh, he was Ra's son and earthly representative. Such a consciousness undoubtedly prompted his rejection of Amon. The young king devoted himself with great abandon to his reform movement, and was only kept from being too precipitous in his reform by the guiding hand of Tiy, his mother. The priests of Amon obviously resented the new art, which had already emerged in the reign of Amenhotep III just as much as the new religion; for one went with the other, and both were inimical to the stereotyped ideas of Amonism. The members of the court, on the other hand, encouraged the reformer, with a

*Photograph by Harry Burton, The Metropolitan Museum of Art*

Rays of the sun with symbols of life pour down upon Ikhnaton and Nefertiti at the Window of Appearances. The partially erased figures of the king and queen lean from the balcony. Relief on wall of Tomb of Ramose, Thebes.

view dictated by expediency rather than intellectual integrity. But theirs was a precarious course in view of the power of the priests. The records show that the king was not above showering gifts upon Ramose and other court officials in payment for their loyalty to him and his new doctrines.

Subject to a diversity of influences — the wisdom of his mother, his own consciousness of Egypt's long history, the ideas of Syrian, Babylonian and Cretan ambassadors at the cosmopolitan court of Thebes, and the advice of his vizier — the youthful king rapidly matured. He received the support of the nobles, and this helps to explain how he was able to effect his revolution despite the power of the Amon hierarchy. When Nefertiti and Amenhotep IV named their first child Meritaton after Aton, to the displeasure of Tiy and the Amon priests, the more or less clandestine activities of the king were openly avowed.

At first there was little trace of monotheism in the new religion. Other gods were tolerated. There was no break with the worship of Ra, who was still revered as " the great God, Lord of Heaven, King of all gods, Ra-Harakhti, rejoicing in the horizon in his name Heat which is in Aton." By the sixth year of his reign, when he was nineteen years of age, Amenhotep's thought was moving farther away from Amonism; but he was still surrounded by all the physical evidences of the power of Amon—on temple walls, pylons, monuments and statues.

The change in religion is vividly illustrated in two reliefs in the tomb of Ramose, Ikhnaton's vizier. This tomb was started while he and the king were still in Thebes. In its first stages at least, the tomb was fashioned in the style of the earlier Eighteenth Dynasty. There are two portraits of Amenhotep IV side by side. The first shows the king seated upon his throne with the goddess Maat (Truth) standing nearby. The sun's rays are not shown and the style of the whole picture is obviously the one which prevailed during the reign of Amenhotep III.

Shortly after the building of this tomb, either before the removal of the court to Amarna or just afterward, Nakht replaced Ramose as vizier. The tomb was prepared during the fourth or fifth year of the reign and, coincidentally with his religious reform, the king directed the artists to turn to the second relief which would be more in keeping with the new religion. The second relief shows the king and Nefertiti standing under the sun-disc. The rays of sunlight end in human hands which bestow the symbol of life upon the royal pair. The king is shown receiving Ramose and other dignitaries. The figures in this second relief emphasize the same curved line and body irregularity seen in Amarna.

The strife that was now to embroil Thebes came not from the complaints of vassal kings in the provinces, but from the palace itself. The disturbing events which occurred six years after the inauguration of the new reign could only have been the work of the young king. Influential as Tiy may have been, and interested as she was in Atonism, it is unreasonable to think that she was party to any violent upset. Her devotion to the sun-god was not strong enough to provoke open revolt from the Amon priesthood. Both Tiy and Horemheb were cool to the new form of worship, but the latter, out of personal loyalty to the pharaoh, did not overtly oppose him. The same can be said of Ay, the priest. Nefertiti grew suspicious of her mother and certainly there was little love lost between them.

The first action of the king, now twenty-one, was to order the construction of a temple to Aton. This temple

was built of sandstone quarried at Silsileh where a tablet was erected containing the following inscription:

> First occurrence of His Majesty's giving command to muster all the workmen from Elephantine to Samhudet, and the leaders of the army, in order to make a great breach for cutting out sandstone, in order to make the sanctuary of Harakhti in his name, "Heat-which-is-in-Aton," in Karnak. Behold the officials, the companions, and the chiefs of the fan-bearers were the chiefs of the quarry-service for the transportation of stone.

How would this be taken by Thebes, stronghold of Amon, whose priesthood was the most powerfully organized group in Egypt? As a matter of fact, no great objection was raised at first by either priests or populace. Thebes had temples for lesser gods and a certain tolerance prevailed even in the citadel of Amon. It was an unexpected occurrence, but no loud protest ensued. After all, it was the privilege of the pharaoh to erect a temple for his favorite god if he so wished. The Silsileh tablet reveals the confusion and hesitancy with which Atonism was regarded. It shows the king worshiping Amon (a gesture to tradition, perhaps), but above this relief the symbolic representation of Aton was portrayed for the first time: the sun-disc with great rays of light extending from it and terminating in human hands, some of which hold the *ankh* or hieroglyphic sign of life. This carving testifies to the king's growing faith in the immanence of the universal sun-god, whose beneficence rules over the activities of men and brings life to all. The sun's energy is the source of all life and the beauty of the natural world. Later, when the devotion to Aton became more fanatical and intolerant, the portrayal of the king bowing before Amon was stricken, but at this juncture some of the conventional ideas still found expression.

*Photograph by Harry Burton, The Metropolitan Museum of Art*

Attendants are in the background as the rays of the sun pour down on Ikhnaton and Nefertiti. Relief on wall of Tomb of Ramose, Thebes.

The Aton temple at Karnak was completely razed in the wholesale destruction of all evidences of Atonism after the death of the heretic king, but many of the stone blocks were later used by Horemheb in the construction of his temple to Amon at Karnak. The reliefs on these stones give us some idea of the size of the building and, what is more important, preserve for us the first artistic expression of the new solar faith.

The naturalistic paintings of birds, plants and animals in the palace art of Amarna bear a close resemblance to those of the palace of Amenhotep III and the Aton temple at Thebes, indicating that Ikhnaton took some of the same painters with him to Akhetaton. The continued presentation in the Theban style is also evident in sculptured human figures.

The " original " style of the Amarna period is eloquently expressed in the colossal statues of Ikhnaton in the Aton temple of Karnak, sculptured just before the abandonment of Thebes. They recall the Osirian mummy-form statues of Queen Hatshepsut at Deir el-Bahri, but pursue a technical and dynamic style of their own. The king is shown alive and reigning, equipped with royal beard, flail, crook and uraeus. The Amarna style is characterized by the elongated face, slanting eyes, protruding lips, long jaw and enlarged abdomen.

Not content with the erection of the Aton temple, the young king decreed that the temple area be called " Brightness of Aton the Great." Then he commanded that Thebes itself, the home of Amon, should be called " The City of the Brightness of Aton." If this were not sufficient cause for open hostility on the part of the powerfully entrenched Theban hierarchy, the pharaoh's next move most assuredly was.

The climax in the transition to Atonism dramatically

occurred when the king changed his name from Amenhotep ("Amon rests") to Ikhnaton ("Aton is satisfied"). The new name was a spectacular symbol of the king's complete denial of Amonism. This break, in the sixth year of the reign, was logical enough, for he knew he could not bear the name of a god whose existence he did not acknowledge. Such a series of events, without parallel in the four thousand years of ancient Egyptian history, constituted an ultimatum. The priestly tolerance of the new cult was at an end. Now the lines were clearly drawn. Both sides knew where they stood and no compromise would be expected. Naturally it took a strong mind to instigate a religious revolution in the face of two thousand years in which the vested religions of Egypt had been thoroughly ingrained into the life and thought of the people.

Ikhnaton's iconoclasm pushed him still further and he next commanded that all Amon temples be closed and all inscriptions containing the name of Amon be erased. Sculptors proceeded at once with the colossal task of chiseling out the name of Amon wherever it appeared — from the statues of kings and nobles, from the walls of temples and even from the top of the glorious obelisk of Queen Hatshepsut at Karnak. The enormity of this undertaking can be appreciated when one considers the countless inscriptions bearing the royal cartouche of the Amenhotep line, all of which had to be chipped out. Ikhnaton's single-minded pursuit of monotheism finally culminated in the elimination of the word "gods" wherever it appeared.

To accomplish the disestablishment of the national god Amon-Ra and abolish the connection between the sacerdotal class and the state was an insurmountable task in any country at any time. But in Egypt, it must be remembered, the kings were not only sons of Amon, they were also deeply indebted to him, for it was he who was responsible for the expulsion of the Hyksos and the conquest of Syria, Nubia and Palestine — gods have always been credited with the achievements of man. Amon upheld the power and authority of the pharaoh in the internal government of Egypt. The priests of Amon were therefore most powerful in the affairs of state and often bent the pharaohs to their will.

One can imagine the consternation of the people to find their immemorial way of life suddenly interrupted, their holy places desecrated, their temples closed and their priests defrocked. No longer could their dead be buried with the ancient rites of Osiris, their protector and judge. And the priests were not the only persons deprived of their means of livelihood — bakers could no longer sell their ceremonial bread at the temple feasts; makers of amulets and charms found themselves without a market; sculptors of Osirian statuettes were out of business; stonecutters and professional scribes could no longer inscribe scenes from the Book of the Dead on monument or papyrus — all were affected by the decree of this king who was no more than a youth. Amonism, like the cult of Osiris, was deeply concerned with death. Death, as a matter of fact, was a major source of revenue. As a result of the closing of the temples in Thebes, thousands of embalmers, mortuary assistants, sculptors and masons suddenly found themselves without work. Some rioting did occur, but Horemheb and his troops were not long in quelling the mob. How long could such a revolution be expected to stand in the face of the growing popular discontent, priestly opposition and the disaffection of the military?

What was the effect of the religious revolution on the common people? Of this we can be certain: Atonism was first and last a religion of the court. Christianity took its rise and flourished among the lower classes, and although it later became a state religion with royal patronage, its roots were deep in the hearts of the people. It was quite the opposite with Atonism, which was instituted by the king and propagated by him among his nobles. As far as we know, it never affected the general public except, perhaps, for the workers and artisans at Amarna. If Atonism had in any way gained the support of the people, it would not have disappeared almost overnight with the death of its founder. Members of the court embraced the new religion either from sincere interest or from expediency, but apparently the king was not interested in the promulgation of Atonism among the common people.

The same was true, for that matter, of Amonism, from which the masses remained completely aloof. It was the lesser gods and the paraphernalia of the Osirian cult that beguiled the mind and heart and daily life of the *fellahin.* If Amonism had played any significant role in the life of the common people, it would have been impossible for any king to overthrow it as easily and quickly as Amenhotep IV did. There was, as has been indicated, a bitter struggle on the part of the priests and those whose livelihood depended on the worship of Amon, but there is no evidence of any rebellion by the great mass of people. The speed and finality with which the change occurred are proof enough that both Amonism and Atonism were confined almost exclusively to the court.

It would be interesting to theorize on the subsequent history of Egypt had Atonism survived long enough to take hold of the affections of the people. Perhaps Atonism was too idealistic and abstract for such a thing to happen. The religion of the young reformer had potentially more to offer the people than the all-too-prosperous state religion of Amon, but it lacked the pomp and pageantry that would appeal to the common people.

The question still persists, however: How did such a young and inexperienced king prevail over the powerful Amon priesthood? It must be remembered that although young and inexperienced, the king was king; he was Amenhotep IV and he came from a powerful line of rulers. In spite of his youth, he clearly possessed unusual personal qualities. Perhaps we should say that his youth *enabled* him to effect this momentous reform. History reveals many examples of signal achievement by young men urged on by burning enthusiasm and utter dedication. Here, in a familiar pattern, was a fanatic who became more fanatical, whose passion for reform gained speed and momentum, as he developed into young manhood. Moreover, he received the support of the Memphis priests, who had never been reconciled to the dominance of the Theban theocracy.

Horemheb, on the other hand, preferred to side with the heretic king rather than with the Amon priesthood — much to the annoyance of Tiy. To the army, a less powerful hierarchy was an unmistakable advantage. In addition, Horemheb hoped to gain certain monopolies previously enjoyed by the priests, such as the gold output of Nubia. The new and younger army officers probably followed Horemheb, but the older and more conservative military men opposed the pacifistic reform. Recognizing that their well-being went hand in hand with the spoils of the empire, the priests of Amon had captured the loyalty of the latter group.

The campaign to obliterate all signs and symbols of a prior faith continued on its relentless course. Ikhnaton now fully perceived his divinely appointed mission as the prophet of Aton to establish the new faith, not only among his own people but also in foreign cities. Some members of the court became loyal devotees of the new cult, but few outside the palace took up the cause. As the atmosphere of the city grew increasingly intolerable, Ikhnaton became convinced that his reform would never flourish in so hostile an environment. The city of Amon had lost its lustre. It became a ghost city, joining hands with the City of the Dead across the river. As the king looked across the plain of Thebes and contemplated the silent mortuary temples of the Amenhotep line, he was filled with remorse. The sullen priests, deprived of their means of livelihood and their prestige, menacingly roamed the city. Why should they not resent the intrusion of this new form of worship that was receiving all the wealth formerly reserved for the Amon temples? Ikhnaton's successful defiance of the priests of Amon was the more surprising in view of their overwhelming political power. They had been strong enough to install Thutmose III against formidable opposition. Why should they not also overcome and dispose of Ikhnaton to replace him with a king more to their liking? Such a possibility had been rendered less likely when Amenhotep III appointed a vizier who was not, for once, also the High Priest. Amenhotep's vizier, Ramose, continued in his post under Ikhnaton, and was, as a matter of fact, one of the first adherents to the new cult. It was Ramose who took charge of the quarrying for the Aton temple, and clearly his conversion was of great strategic significance in a court which, almost as a matter of course, followed the lead of its vizier.

The situation was none the less insufferable and the king became desperate. He was compelled to find a more fertile soil in which to plant and nourish the faith of Aton, a place uncontaminated by the multifarious gods of Egypt. Perhaps by abandoning Thebes and building another capital he could reduce the prestige of Amonism. At least his plans would not be hampered by its overpowering presence. So Ikhnaton, in the sixth year of his reign, made the momentous decision to leave Thebes forever.

# V The Dream City

On a certain day in the year 1369 B.C. watchers on the shore observed the unusual sight of a well-nigh endless procession of barges floating down the Nile. The golden prow of the leading barque glistened in the brilliant Egyptian sun. This was the royal ship — and royalty was on board. Ikhnaton was sailing into exile to build his dream city, "The City of the Horizon of Aton." Accompanying him were the beautiful Nefertiti, the princesses Meritaton, Maketaton and Ankhsenpaton, Ay, chief counselor of the king, Kenofer, an artist, Ramose, the royal vizier, Thutmose, the chief sculptor, and Nakht, a priest who was to succeed Ramose as vizier shortly after the settlement at Amarna, as well as engineers, architects and builders. A gay flotilla of a hundred vessels followed the royal barge down the river.

For several days the barges descended the great river. Each succeeding day of the voyage brought increased eagerness to see the new city. The party spent the last night of the trip a few miles up the river from the new site so that their arrival would dramatically coincide with the rising of the sun over the eastern cliffs. Now the leading boat rounded the bend. Ikhnaton caught sight of the columns and shining walls of the half-finished palace, the colored pennants flying in salute from the Aton Temple, and the King's House. Thutmose, Bek and the engineers had done

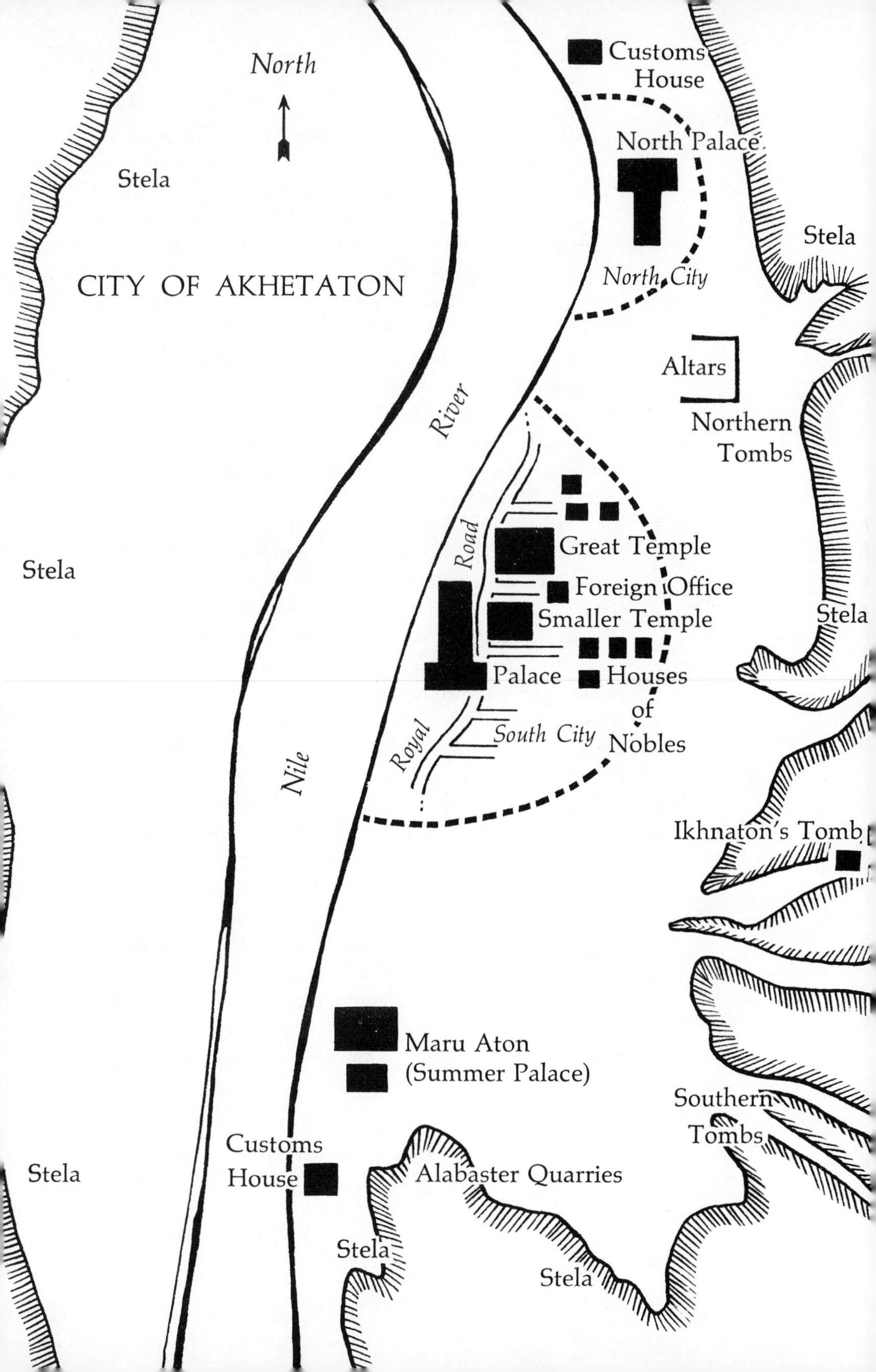
North
CITY OF AKHETATON
Stela
Customs House
North Palace
Stela
North City
Altars
Northern Tombs
River
Road
Great Temple
Foreign Office
Smaller Temple
Stela
Stela
Palace
Houses of Nobles
Royal
South City
Nile
Ikhnaton's Tomb
Maru Aton (Summer Palace)
Southern Tombs
Customs House
Stela
Alabaster Quarries
Stela
Stela

their work well, and the king was pleased. The royal barge was fastened to the wharf, and the newcomers were greeted by the army officers, priests and workers: " Life, health and strength! " The procession filed past the crowd on the dock, climbed the steps to the palm grove, and entered the cool rooms of the palace. After resting a while, Ikhnaton and his wife crossed the bridge which connected the Palace with the King's House and paused at the Window of Appearances, where they would later hold audiences and bestow honors. From this high point, the king commanded a view of the whole site of the new city — from the river to the cliffs and from what would soon be the Customs House at the northern entrance to Maru-Aton at the southern boundary.

Here at Akhetaton all was new. There was nothing to evoke the weighty past, the twenty thousand priests of Amon, the dark sanctuaries of Karnak. Continuing to the King's House, the king and queen prepared to enter the temple for the first Aton ceremony. Carrying floral tributes, they proceeded to the sanctuary accompanied by priests and musicians. For his new capital, Ikhnaton had chosen a peaceful, virgin site about three hundred miles north of Thebes at a point where the eastern cliffs retreat from the river in semicircular fashion for about six miles, leaving a plain some three miles wide between the river and the hills. This plain, protected on three sides by cliffs, was an ideal location for the new city. Previously, Ikhnaton and his engineers had spent several days on a demarcation expedition to set up boundary stelae. The stelae defined the larger domain of the Aton district, which also included the plain on the western bank of the Nile, all of which measured some eight miles in length and from twelve to eighteen miles east to west. The city proper occupied the bay in the hills on the east bank and was six miles long and three

*Egypt Exploration Society, London*

Boundary Stele of Ikhnaton. From Tell el-Amarna. Shows royal family under sun-disc with rays.

miles wide. Not all of this area, of course, was occupied. When completed, Akhetaton stretched along the river for five miles and backward toward the hills only for a half mile, utilizing the fertile strip bordering the river.

Fortunately, fourteen of the boundary stelae remain intact, one of them twenty-six feet high. The actual founding of the city is mentioned in the following inscription on one of the stelae:

> On this day one was in Akhetaton in the pavilion of woven stuff which his majesty made in Akhetaton, the name of which is: "Aton-is-Satisfied." His majesty appeared upon a great chariot of electrum, like Aton, when he rises in the horizon; he filled the Two Lands with his loveliness. On beginning the goodly way to Akhetaton, at the first exploration of it which his majesty made, in order to found it as a monument to Aton, according to the command of his father Aton, who is given life forever and ever; in order to make for him a monument in its midst. One caused that a great oblation should be offered, consisting of bread, beer, oxen, calves, cattle, fowl, wine, gold, incense, all beautiful flowers. On this day was founded Akhetaton for the living Aton, that favor and love might be received on behalf of King Ikhnaton.

The oath of the king that he would never pass beyond the boundaries of the Holy City is recorded on the stelae of all four cardinal points.

> His majesty raised his hand to heaven, to him who made him, even Aton, saying: " This is my testimony, forever, and this is my witness forever, this landmark. . . . I have made Akhetaton for my father as a dwelling for — — —. I have demarked Akhetaton on its south, on its north, on its west, on its east. I shall not pass beyond the southern landmark of Akhetaton toward the south, nor shall I pass beyond the northern landmark of Akhetaton toward the north. . . . He has made its circuit for his own — — —; he hath made his altar in its midst, whereon I make offering to him; this is it.

How literally this vow is to be interpreted is uncertain, but such an oath has never been found on any other ancient boundary inscription. During the two years of building, Ikhnaton may have returned at times to Thebes, but without doubt, by the eighth year of his reign he and his queen had taken up permanent residence in Amarna. They never left the city again. Queen Tiy probably did not approve of the removal of the court to the new city and continued to live in Thebes, visiting Akhetaton only occasionally,

A surviving tablet is inscribed with a prohibition against the blasphemy of worshiping any god but Aton, and so guarded the sancity of the city. All was dedicated to Aton: " Now, as for the area within the four landmarks, from the eastern mountain to the western mountain of Akhetaton opposite, it belongs to my father, Aton, who is given life, forever and ever; whether mountains, or cliffs, or marshes, or uplands, or fields, or waters, or towns, or shores, or people, or cattle, or trees, or anything which Aton, my father, has made."

Finally, provision was made for the burial of the king and his queen.

> There shall be made for me a sepulchre in the Orient mountain; my burial shall be made there in the multitude of jubilees which Aton, my father, hath ordained for me, and the burial of the chief wife of the king (Nefertiti) shall be made therein in that multitude of years . . . and the burial of the king's daughter, Meritaton, shall be made in it in that multitude of years. If I die in any town of the north, south, west, or Orient, in the multitude of years, I will be brought, and my burial made in Akhetaton. If the Great Queen (Nefertiti), who lives, die in any town of north, south, west, or Orient, in the multitude of years, she shall be brought and buried in Akhetaton. If the king's daughter, Meritaton, die in any town of north, south, west, or Orient, she shall be brought and buried in Akhetaton.

Here, under the shelter of the cliffs by the life-giving river, arose within two years Ikhnaton's dream city, a city of unsurpassed beauty, a city of temples, palaces, gardens, public buildings and spacious quays. Bek, the royal architect, was commissioned to procure the stone from Assuan and build the three temples: one for Ikhnaton, one for the queen mother, Tiy, and one for the princess Baketaton, her daughter. These were constructed in the north-central section of the city, near the river. Nearby rose the palace of the pharaoh and the home of the nobles. Further to the east and south were the royal tombs and those of the priests.

The city was described by one of the nobles:

> Akhetaton, great in loveliness, mistress of pleasant ceremonies, rich in possessions, the offerings of Re in her midst. At the sight of her beauty there is rejoicing. She is lovely and beautiful; when one sees her it is like a glimpse of heaven. Her number cannot be calculated. When the Aton rises in her he fills her with his rays and he embraces his beloved son, son of eternity, who came forth from Aton and offers the earth to him who placed him on his throne, causing the earth to belong to him who made him.

Several stelae indicate that the city was completed by the eighth year of the reign and that the court, with all official documents and personnel, had soon after been transferred from Thebes. The three main thoroughfares ran north and south and were intersected at right angles by several other streets. The main street, or King's Way, with the river on one side and the chief buildings on the other, started at Maru-Aton, the pleasure palace, and continued north past the Royal House, the Central Palace, the Great Temple, the North Palace and came to an end in the North City. Parallel to the King's Way ran High Priest Street, bordered by the mansions of the nobles, priests and

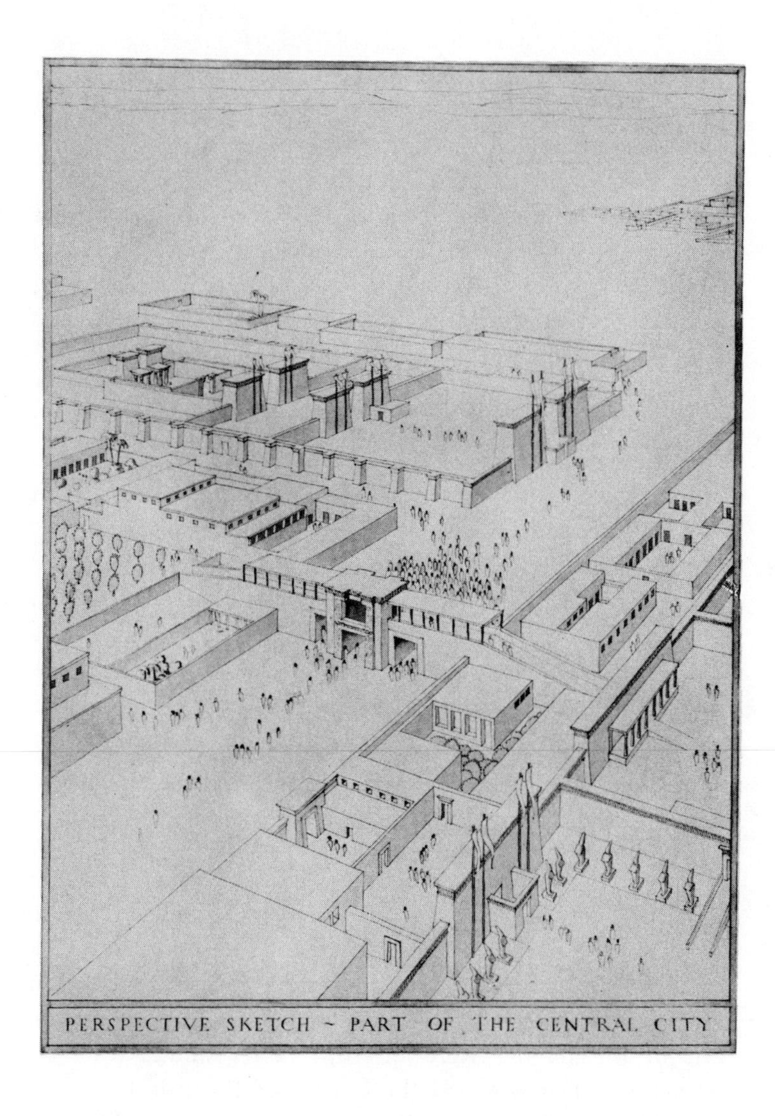


*Egypt Exploration Society, London*

Reconstruction of central quarter of Amarna, showing the Royal Road, bisecting the central area; the bridge connecting the King's House and Royal Chapel (left) and the Great Palace and Harems (right). In the center of the bridge is the Window of Appearances.

government officials. Some of the estates in the North City had not yet been completed when the city was abandoned some eighteen years later.

The central section of Amarna was carefully planned. It consisted of the Great Temple, the Royal Magazines, the Hall of Foreign Tribute, houses of the priests, the royal estate, the foreign office, the " House of Life," where young scribes learned the art of writing and administration, houses of clerks, police barracks, armory and parade grounds.

The Great Temple was planned by Ikhnaton to be the " mother church " for Atonism the world over. The enclosure measured a half-mile in length and three hundred and fifty yards in width, and was surrounded by a high wall. An avenue of sphinxes led to the House of Rejoicing, a smaller temple with two rows of columns flanking the center aisle. At the end of each colonnade stood a carved limestone altar. Beyond this building, a ramp led to the Gem-Aton (The Finding of Aton). The inner court was open to the sky, permitting worship in the open air under the sun. The preliminary temples and the sanctuary itself were light, airy and cheerful in contrast to previous Egyptian temples, with their dark and mysterious chambers. Gem-Aton was composed of a great multitude of courts, passageways, ramps and altars. Mounting finally a long flight of stairs, the worshiper stood before the awesome high altar. Farther to the east lay the inner sanctuary, with an imposing facade and two tremendous pylons. Each pylon supported five masts from which fluttered brilliant pennants. Within the temple were offering tables and statues of Ikhnaton. Nearby stood the houses of the priests.

The temple contained no image of god, and Atonism depended upon no esoteric rites or elaborate secret ceremonies. However, the ritual did include offerings of food and wine. These offerings were consecrated by the king and queen after they had performed the rite of lustration and had burned the incense. The most prominent feature of the ceremony was music. A permanent choir and orchestra were attached to the temple and performed several hours each day. A special group of male chanters sang during the consecration of the offerings. Simultaneously, female musicians outside the temple played on tambourines and waved palm branches. Encircling the worship area were several small chapels, each leading to a series of gateways that opened on to six courts with temple buildings decorated in gay colors.

Worship was conducted at sunrise and sunset when the king and queen, or priests, officiated at the temple ceremony with the singing of the two hymns. "Thy rising is beautiful in the horizon of heaven, O living Aton, who givest life. Shining from the eastern horizon, Thou fillest Egypt with thy beauty. . . . Thy setting is beautiful, O living Aton, who guidest all countries that they make praise at thy dawning and at thy setting."

But the worship of Aton was not confined to the temple. It was in the gardens and groves of Amarna that the pharaoh exclaimed: "O Lord, how manifold are thy works! The whole land is in joy because of thee. All that thou hast made leaps before thee. Eyes have life at the sight of thy beauty; hearts have health when the Aton shines. There is no poverty for him who hath set thee in his heart."

Little occult mystery clung to the worship of Amarna. The priests were not ascetics, but lovers of truth and beauty. Ikhnaton discarded all magic — the tedious formulae for safe passage into the realm of Osiris, as well as the innumerable spirits, demigods, incantations and bogies. References in Atonism to death and the hereafter took on a spiritual meaning: the desire to be well remembered on earth and a prayer for the continuation of the light of Aton in the soul.

The Aton religion was always called " The Teaching " and was never otherwise designated. This suggests that the king himself taught his followers the doctrine of the Aton. With the new religion firmly established in the City of the Horizon, Ikhnaton appointed Meryra " High Priest of the Aton," in order to have more time to devote to state duties and to propagating the cult throughout the rest of Egypt. Meryra had been an early convert to Atonism but little is known of his career, though his investiture is described on the wall of his tomb at Amarna. In this scene, the king and queen are standing at a window of the palace balcony which is decorated with garlands of lotus flowers. Colored pennants flutter from the flagstaffs of the palace. A group of courtiers and spectators stand before the window. Ikhnaton leans over the balcony and addresses the priest: " Behold, I make thee High Priest of the Aton for me in the Temple of the Aton in the City of the Horizon. I do this for my love of thee and I say unto thee: 'O my servant, who listens to my teaching, my heart is delighted with all that thou hast·done. I give thee this office, and I say unto thee, thou shalt eat the food of Pharaoh, the Lord, in the Temple of Aton.' "

The high priest replies: " Abundant are the rewards which the Aton knows to give when his heart is pleased." The king installs Meryra in the office of high priest and then presents him with precious gifts. In the background stand the chariot of the priest, fan-bearers and dancers. Girls throw flowers in his path as Meryra is carried away on the shoulders of his friends.

The wall decoration continues with the royal procession to the temple. The king drives his chariot through the city streets, followed by the queen and princesses,

*Egypt Exploration Society, London*

Royal Palace in central district of Amarna. Reconstruction shows Great Pillared Hall (extreme right), main rooms of palace (center) and gardens and colossal statues (left).

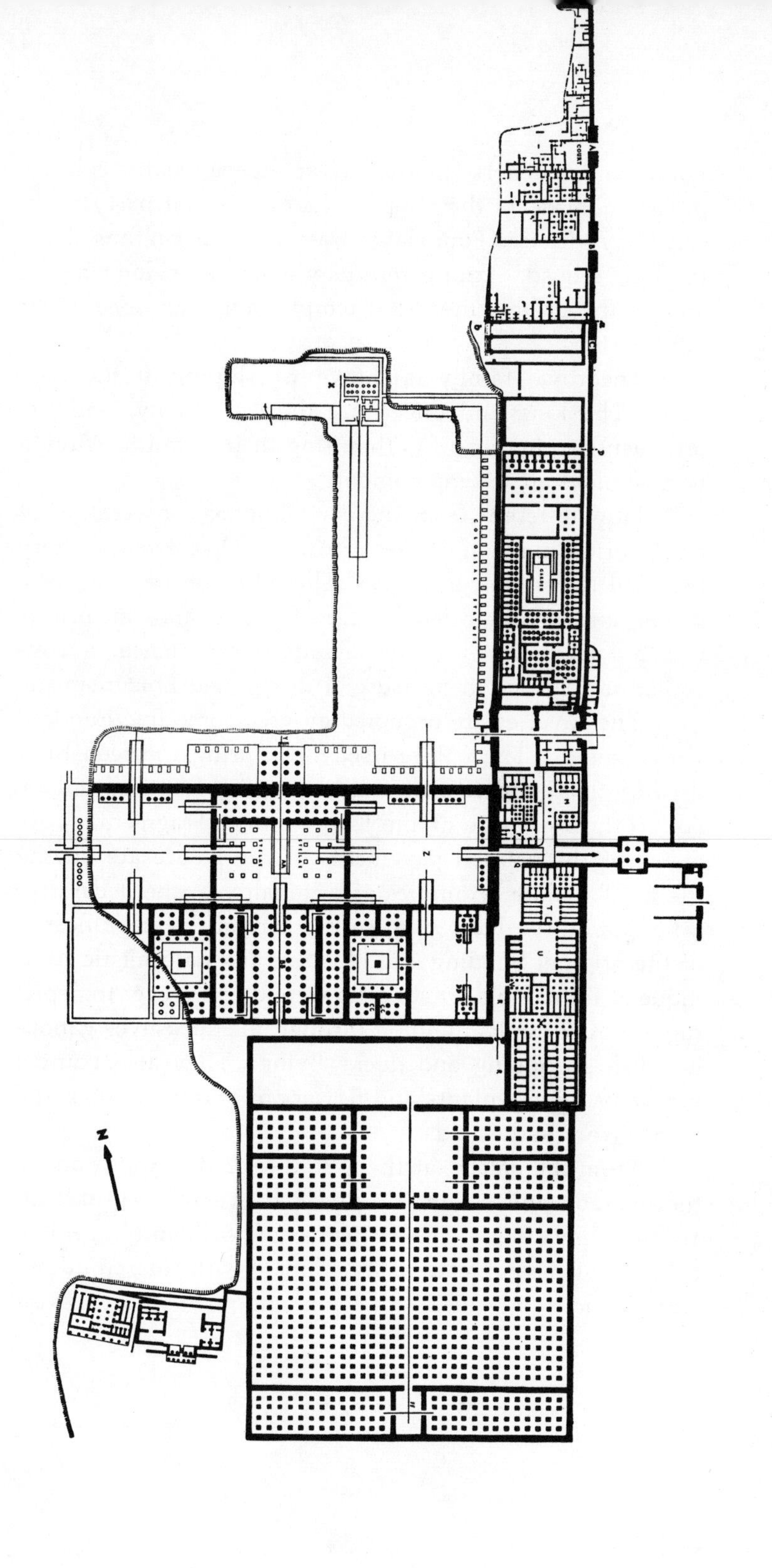

nobles and courtiers. Soldiers clear the way as the colorful processional nears the temple where the royal party is received by Meryra. Four slaves waft huge ostrich fans above the king's head. Trumpeters play a salute on long horns, and as the group enters the temple, musicians beat their tambourines.

The royal family is shown worshiping at the high altar. The king and queen are dressed simply, with no ornaments or jewelry. As they sing their hymn to Aton, a harpist plays an accompaniment.

How different from the conventional consecration of a high priest in the mysteries of Amon! No solemn mystery here; all is gay and informal. This pharaoh believed in a simple and joyous religion. Life for him and his priests was an aesthetic — not an ascetic — experience, a controlled indulgence in pleasure, a disciplined Epicureanism.

The royal estate occupied an area some five hundred yards square. The palace itself, measuring fourteen hundred by five hundred feet and having five hundred pillars, lay on the west side of the King's Way. Fragmentary remains of the painted pavements of the palace are among the most striking examples of originality in the decorative art of antiquity. They give us just a hint of the magnificence of the original building and illustrate the naturalistic technique of Ikhnaton's artists, who were the first ever to depict rapid motion: bulls jumping through the air, calves galloping, fish swimming and ducks flying. They also painted everyday things: plants and flowers of many varieties and men at work in the fields.

From the palace, at the Window of the Appearances, the pharaoh and his family presided over official and informal functions. The remains of brilliantly painted columns of the palm frond style, inlaid with colored glazes, were found in the queen's pavilion, and farther north, exca-

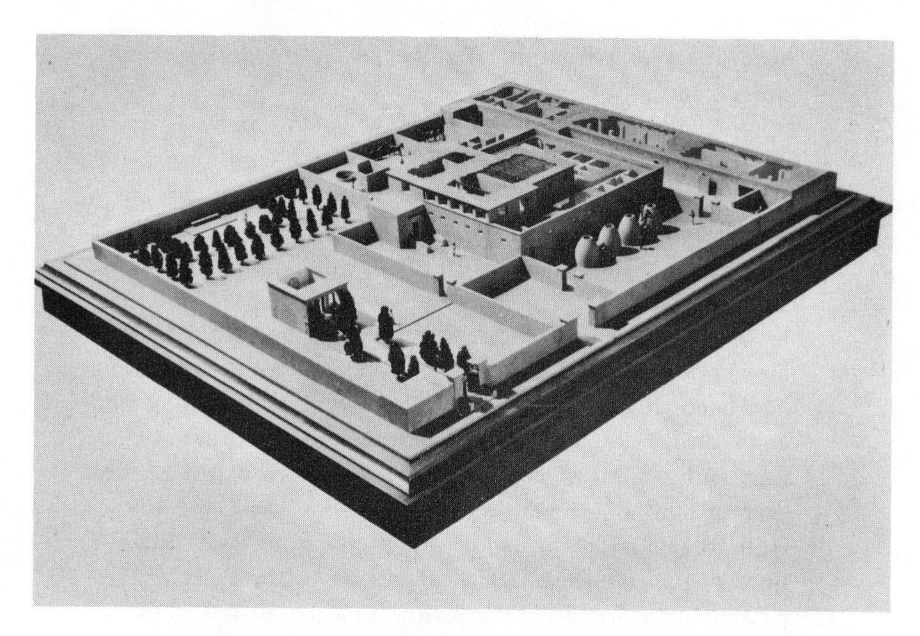

*The Oriental Institute, The University of Chicago*

Model of the house and estate of a Tell el-Amarna nobleman. About 1375–1350 B.C.

vation unearthed many fragments of limestone relief as well as the death mask of Ikhnaton. Around the northern end of the royal estate ran a formal terraced garden, to the right of which stood the house of the king. The living room of the house contained forty-two columns in six rows. Another hall of twenty columns led to private quarters of the king and queen. The walls of the palace were covered with continuous frescoes, which were discovered by Petrie in 1891. Back of the house were the royal magazines housing sealed wine jars, sacks of valuable objects, bales of cloth, grain, bread, spices, ancestral treasures and objects of foreign tribute. Connected to the king's house was a private temple called Hat-Aton, which was patterned throughout after the Great Temple. To the south stood the priests' quarters and the sacred lake.

At the extreme southern end of Amarna was Maru-Aton, a royal park or grove dedicated to Aton and to the enjoyment of the outdoor life. Within this enclosure a temple had been built, thus combining the appreciation of the beauties of nature with the worship of their divine source. Maru-Aton consisted of two main areas, the smaller of which contained beautiful flower beds, a lake and a reception hall. In the larger section another pleasure lake had been dug. One hundred and twenty yards long and sixty yards wide, the lake was surrounded by ornate buildings and a plant aquarium. Near the shore was a rectangular island of flowers and shrubs. Crossing the bridge from the island, guests of the pharaoh walked down a flowery path and through a colonnade to the temple. The pavements were decorated with frescoed panels showing marsh scenes of cattle jumping among papyrus brakes, and startled ducks taking flight. Still another royal residence, the North Palace, contained gardens, aviaries, enclosure for animals, a bird sanctuary and beautiful frescoes of bird life. One can picture Ikhnaton and Nefertiti entertaining their friends and visitors in this secluded and peaceful retreat.

In the first two years at Amarna, the land was allotted and the estates laid out along the main streets. A typical middle-class house occupied an area of two hundred by one hundred fifty feet. The front entrance was flanked by two pylon towers. An avenue of trees led to the private open-air chapel. Behind the chapel ran a formal garden and an artificial lake or pool. The house itself consisted of a large living room surrounded by guest rooms and storerooms. The front door had a stone frame and the name of the owner was inscribed on the lintel. The roof of the house was supported by wooden columns set in stone. A corridor led from the

*Cairo Museum*

Excavation of northern city, Tell el-Amarna.

central room to the sitting room, bedrooms and bathrooms. The decoration of a private house generally consisted of a formal frieze of flowers and birds and hanging garlands. The servants' quarters, ovens and kitchen were separate and always on the east side of the house to avoid the prevailing west wind, and next to these were the stables. Unlike most of the Egyptian buildings, which were made of stone, the public buildings and houses of Amarna were made of mud-brick, which lasted a long time in the extremely dry climate.

Just south of the royal estate stood the homes of the city officials, the most elaborate of which were those of Nakht, the new vizier, who had replaced Ramose shortly after the occupation of Amarna; Panhesy, the Chief Servitor of the god; and Ranefer, Master of Horse. Here also lived Thutmose, sculptor of the famous head of Nefertiti. Still further to the south rose the faience and glass factories.

As the population increased, the city expanded toward the north. This section was called the North Suburb and was inhabited by minor officials and middle-class citizens. It also boasted the North Palace, with its exquisite wall paintings of bird life and marsh scenes. Beyond the North Suburb was the North City, the seat of the queen's palace, to which Nerfertiti retired after the death of her husband. The Customs House (used for the unloading and inspection of material entering from the north) was located at the extreme northern point of Amarna. A similar office was built at the southern end.

To the Egyptian his " House of Eternity " was even more important than his earthly home. Not the least significant feature of Amarna therefore was the necropolis. The rock tombs of the nobles were cut in the surrounding eastern cliffs. The importance of these tombs lies not in the recovery of mummies, for none has ever been found, but in the colored wall paintings and low reliefs. In some instances the bodies of the officials and priests were probably removed to Thebes when Amarna was deserted by the court. Like the Theban tombs, all have been defaced, some deliberately during the destruction of the city by the reactionary forces, others by later tomb robbers. It is through the tomb reliefs that we become intimately acquainted with the life and culture of Amarna — the public ceremonies, the private life of the royal family and the visits of foreign dignitaries. Even more important, however, are the hymns and texts relating to the new religion of Ikhnaton.

From the tomb paintings we can reconstruct two events which took place during the twelfth year of the reign. One was a ceremony for the receiving of tribute from foreign states. The king and queen are pictured seated in a gold palanquin and, although the ceremony was a dignified state function, Nefertiti has her arm around her husband's waist and leans her head on his shoulder. The palanquin, in the form of a double throne, is borne on the shoulders of the court nobles. A priest, swinging an incense burner, precedes king and queen in the procession while the princesses follow on foot. The ceremony itself takes place at a pavilion where the viceroys of the vassal states are received. Bearded Asiatics from Syria bring specially bred horses, chariots, spears, shields, ivory tusks, precious stones, metal vessels and wild animals. Ornate vases from Crete, ostrich feathers from Libya, gold bars from the Sudan are all laid in front of the pavilion. Finally, captive slaves are led by, and it is significant that they are not manacled and have not been subjected to torture.

The second event was a visit of the queen mother to Amarna. Although she had originally been sympathetic toward Atonism and had encouraged Ikhnaton in his revolutionary movement, Tiy had not favored the building of Akhetaton and had therefore remained in Thebes. For the first few years of the reign in Thebes she had enjoyed the prestige and power of a pharaoh but the removal of the court to Amarna changed everything for her, and she must have missed the luxury and power she once enjoyed. Ikhnaton built a palace for her in the City of the Horizon but only on rare occasions did she visit her son.

One of these state visits occurred in the twelfth year of the reign, when she was about fifty-five years of age and her daughter, Baketaton, twelve. The occasion was one of great pomp. The artist shows Ikhnaton, Nefertiti, Tiy, Baketaton, Meritaton and Akhnsenpaton seated at table. The king and queen are simply dressed in contrast to Tiy who wears an ornately beautiful robe and an elaborate wig of gold on top of which rests a crown of the disc, two horns, two tall plumes and two serpents. The tables are laden with every variety of meat, vegetable, fruit and pastry. Jugs of wine stand near the tables. While the guests enjoy the feast, two small orchestras provide music. Courtiers stand around the hall at a respectful distance.

A second scene shows the same group at an evening reception in honor of the queen mother. On this occasion the refreshments consist mostly of wine and fruit. The hall is illuminated by several tall lamps. Waiters with napkins on their arms move about among the guests.

A third relief in the same tomb describes the dowager's visit to the " Shade of the Sun ", a private temple built expressly for her. This temple resembles the others and is gayly decorated with garlands and flowers. As the royal family enters the temple, accompanied by the nobles and court officials, they are greeted by the cheering people.

The tomb of Mahu, chief of the Mazoi, the city police, is one of the best preserved in Amarna and contains a number of impressive reliefs: the vizier running along beside the royal chariot as it leaves the temple, the inspection of sentry posts by Mahu and the king, Mahu in the storehouse presenting a requisition from the vizier for supplies, the capture of foreign spies by Mahu and the appearance of the prisoners before the vizier. All of these are sculptured in exquisite detail. The wonder is that the quarriers, engineers, draftsmen, artists and sculptors were able to complete so many tombs in such a short time.

It would be a mistake, however, to think that Akhetaton was an isolated Shangri-La where the king and his entourage spent their days in uninterrupted contemplation of Aton. It was still the capital of the empire and Ikhnaton was still the pharaoh. Messengers and ambassadors from foreign lands were frequent visitors. Some of these emissaries brought disquieting reports of intrigue and revolt abroad. A governor in Syria wrote that his city was in danger of invasion and that he had not heard from the king of Egypt for many years. Ebed-Hepa, governor of Jerusalem, wrote frequently to Ikhnaton warning him that unless troops were dispatched soon Palestine would fall to the Habiri. It is not clear whether the name Habiri (Apiru) refers to a Hebrew tribe or not. If so, it would seem that some of the Hebrews were invading Canaan long before Joshua's conquest. Two of his letters read as follows:

To the king, my lord, speak, saying, Ebed-Hepa, thy servant — at the feet of my lord, the king, seven times and seven times I prostrate myself. What have I done to the king, my lord? They slander and misrepresent me before the king, my lord, saying: Ebed-Hepa is disloyal to the king, his lord. Behold — neither my father nor my mother set me in this place; the arm of the mighty king caused me to enter into the house of my father. Why should I commit rebellion against the king, my lord? As long as the king, my lord, lives I will say unto the governor of the king, my lord: " Why dost thou love the Habiri and hate the prefects? " But thus he misrepresents me before the king, my lord. Now I say, " Lost are the lands of the king, my lord." So he misrepresents me to the king, my lord. But let the king, my lord, know after the king, my lord, set guards, Ienhamu took them all . . . Egypt . . . of the king, my lord; there are no guards there. Then may the king care for his land! May the king care for his land! Separated are all the lands from the king. Ilimilku has destroyed all the country of the king; so may the king, my lord, care for his land! I say: " I will enter the presence of the king, my lord, and I will behold the eye of the king, my lord," but the enemy is more mighty than I, and I am not able to enter into the presence of the king, my lord. So may it seem right to the king . . . may he send guards, and I will enter in and will behold the eyes of the king, my lord! And so long as the king, my lord, lives, so long as the governors are withdrawn, I will say: " Perished are the lands of the king." Thou doest not hearken to me! All the prefects have perished; there is left no prefect to the king, my lord! May the king turn his face toward mercenaries, so that there may come forth mercenaries of the king, my lord. There are no lands left to the king, my lord. The Habiri plunder all the countries of the king. If there are mercenaries in this year, then there will be left countries of the king, my lord. If there are no mercenaries, the countries of the king will be lost. Unto the scribe of the king, my lord, saying: " Ebed-Hepa, thy servant. Take beautiful words to the king, my lord! Lost are all the lands of the king, my lord."

Verily, this land of Urusalim, neither my father nor my mother has given it to me; the mighty hand of the king gave it to me. . . . Verily, the king has set his name upon the land of Urusalim for ever. Therefore he cannot abandon the lands of Urusalim.

Let the king care for his land. The land of the king will be lost. All of it will be taken from me; there is hostility to me. . . . But now the Habiri are taking the cities of the king. . . . If there are no archers this year, then let the king send a deputy that he may take me to himself together with my brothers and we die with the king, our lord.

Rib-Addi, governor of Byblos in Phoenicia, wrote of an impending attack upon his land by the Amurru (Amorites) under Aziru, and informed the king that he himself had fled to Berytus (Beirut). One of the fifty or more urgent appeals received from Rib-Addi runs as follows:

Rib-Addi spoke to the king, his lord, the Sun-god of the lands. Beneath the feet of the king, my lord, seven times, and seven times I fall. I have written repeatedly for garrison troops, but they were not given, and the king did not listen to the words of his servant. And I sent my courier to the palace, but he returned empty-handed — he had no garrison troops. And when the people of my house saw that silver was not given, they ridiculed me like the governors, my brethren, and they despised me.

Further, I went to Hamuniri, and my younger brother is estranging Byblos in order to give the city to the sons of 'Abdu-Ashirta. When my brother saw that my courier came out from Egypt empty-handed, that there were no garrison troops with him, he despised me, and so he committed a crime and drove me from the city. Let the king not restrain himself at the deed of this dog!

Behold, I cannot enter the land of Egypt. I am an old man, there is grievous illness in my body, and the king, my lord, knows that the gods of Byblos are holy, and the illness is severe; and my sin I have redeemed by a vow from the gods, so I have not entered the presence of the king, my lord.

But behold, my son, the servant of the king, my lord, I have sent before the king, my lord. Let the king hear the words of his servant, and let the king, my lord, give archers, and let them take Byblos, lest rebellious troops and the sons of 'Abdu-Ashirta enter it and the archers of the king, my lord, then need to capture it by force. Behold, many are the people who love me in the city; few are the rebels in it. When an army of archers goes out and they hear about the day of its arrival, then the city will return to the king, my lord. Let my lord know that I would die for him. When I am in the city, I will protect it for my lord, and my heart is fixed on the king, my lord; I will not give the city to the sons of 'Abdu-Ashirta. So my brother has estranged the city in order to give it to the sons of 'Abdu-Ashirta. Let the king, my lord, not hold back from the city. Verily, there is very much silver and gold within it; in its temple there is much wealth. If they take it, let the king my lord do as he please with his servant, but let him give the city Buruzilim for my dwelling place — behold, I am now with Hamuniri — since there is left but one city, namely Buruzilim. The sons of 'Abdu-Ashirta were hostile, and I was afraid. When I went to Hamuniri because of the sons of 'Abdu-Ashirta when they were powerful against me and there was no breath of the mouth of the king to me, then I said to my lord: " Behold our city Byblos! There is much wealth of the king in it, the property of our forefathers. If the king does not intervene for the city, all the cities of the land of Canaan will not longer be his. Let the king not ignore this deed! "

Now I have sent thy servant, my son, to the king, my lord; let the king quickly send him back with troops to take the city. If the king, my lord, be gracious to me and return me to the city, then I will guard it as before for the king, my lord. If the king, my lord, does not bring me back into it, then . . . the city from Buruzilim . . . may he do as he please to his servant. . . . Forsake . . . Hamuniri . . . until when shall I remain with him?

May the king, my lord, hear the words of his servant quickly and send troops quickly to take the city. Let the king not ignore this grievous deed which was done to the lands of the king, my lord; but let the king rush archers to take the city immediately. If it is said to the king concerning the city: " The city is strong," it is not strong against the warriors of the king, my lord.

Intervention in these critical areas would mean war, and Ikhnaton preferred peace to imperialism. The result was a gradual nibbling away of the vassal states and the beginning of the Asiatic aggression that led ultimately to the dissolution of the Egyptian empire. At this time Syria and Palestine were gradually passing out of Egyptian dominion as the Hittites, the Amorites, and the Habiri continued to gain control. Absorbed as he was in the promotion of his religious reform, Ikhnaton either did not realize the seriousness of the situation until it was too late, or deliberately ignored it. The only thing that mattered to the king now was his devotion to Aton.

# VI O Living Aton

Curiously enough, most of our information concerning the true nature of Atonism comes from reliefs in the tombs of the nobles, rather than from the ruins of the temples. The two great hymns to Aton, composed by Ikhnaton for his family devotions and temple services, are still preserved. The first and longer hymn is one of the most profound expressions of the truly religious spirit in all history, with its frank and ecstatic appreciation of the natural world, its universalistic conception of Aton as the creator and sustainer of all life and its deep mysticism. This hymn was inscribed upon the tomb of Ay.

## HYMN TO ATON

*Introduction*

A Hymn of praise of Harakhti, the living one exalted in the Eastern Horizon in his name of Shu-who-is-in-the-Aton, who liveth for ever and ever, the living and great Aton, he who is in the Sed Festival, the Lord of the Globe, the Lord of the Disc, the Lord of Heaven, the Lord of Earth, the Lord of the House of Aton in Akhetaton, of the King of the South and the North, who liveth in Truth, Lord of the Two Lands, Nefer-kheperu-Ra-Ua-en-Ra, the Son of Ra, who liveth in Truth, Lord of Diadems, Akhenaton, great in the duration of his life, and of the Great Royal Wife whom he loveth, Lady of the Two Lands, Nefer-neferu-Aton, Nofreteti, who liveth in health and youth for ever and ever.

### *Universal Splendor and Power of Aton*

Thou dawnest beautifully in the horizon of the sky,
O living Aton who was the Beginning of life!
When thou didst rise in the eastern horizon,
Thou didst fill every land with thy beauty.
Thou art beautiful, great, glittering, high over every land,
Thy rays, they encompass the lands, even to the end of all that
thou hast made.
Thou art Re, and thou penetratest to the very end of them;
Thou bindest them for thy beloved son.
Though thou art far away, thy rays are upon earth;
Though thou art in the faces of men, thy footsteps are unseen.

### *Night and Man*

When thou settest in the western horizon of the sky,
The earth is in darkness like death.
They sleep in their chambers,
Their heads are wrapped up,
Their nostrils are stopped,
And none seeth the other,
While all their things are stolen,
Which are under their heads,
And they know it not.

### *Night and Animals*

Every lion cometh forth from his den,
All serpents, they sting.
Darkness broods,
The world is in silence,
He that made them resteth in his horizon.

### *Day and Man*

Bright is the earth when thou risest in the horizon;
When thou shinest as Aton by day
Thou drivest away the darkness.
When thou sendest forth thy rays,
The Two Lands are in daily festivity.
Men waken and stand upon their feet
When thou hast raised them up.
Their limbs bathed, they take their clothing,
Their arms uplifted in adoration to thy dawning.
Then in all the world they do their work.

### *Day and the Animals and Plants*

All cattle rest upon their pasturage,
The trees and the plants flourish,
The birds flutter in their marshes,
Their wings uplifted in adoration to thee.
All creatures that fly or alight.
They live when thou hast shone upon them.

### *Day and the Waters*

The barques sail upstream and downstream alike.
Every highway is open because thou dawnest.
The fish in the river leap up before thee.
Thy rays are in the midst of the great green sea.

### *Creation of Man*

Creator of the germ in woman,
Who makest seed into men,
Making alive the son in the body of his mother,
Soothing him that he may not weep,
Nurse even in the womb,
Giver of breath to sustain alive every one that he maketh!
When he descendeth from the body on the day of his birth,
Thou openest his mouth altogether,
Thou suppliest his necessities.

*Creation of Animals*

When the fledgling in the egg chirps in the shell,
Thou givest him breath in the midst of it to preserve him alive.
Thou hast made for him his term in the egg, for breaking it.
He cometh forth from the egg to chirp with all his might;
He goeth about upon his two feet
When he cometh forth therefrom.

*Universal Creation* 

How manifold are thy works!
They are hidden before men
O sole God, beside whom there is no other.
Thou didst create the earth according to thy heart.
While thou wast alone:
Even men, all herds of cattle and the antelopes;
All that are upon the earth,
That go about upon their feet;
They that are on high,
That fly with their wings.
The highland countries, Syria and Kush,
And the land of Egypt;
Thou settest every man into his place,
Thou suppliest their necessities,
Every one has his food,
And his days are reckoned.
The tongues are divers in speech,
Their forms likewise and their skins are distinguished,
For thou makest different the strangers.

*Watering the Earth in Egypt and Abroad*

Thou makest the Nile in the Nether World,
Thou bringest it as thou desirest,
To preserve alive the people of Egypt.
For thou hast made them for thyself,
Thou lord of them all, who weariest thyself for them;
Thou lord of every land, who risest for them,

Thou Sun of day, great in glory,
All the distant highland countries,
Thou makest also their life,
Thou didst set a Nile in the sky.
When it falleth for them,
It maketh waves upon the mountains,
Like the great green sea,
Watering their fields in their towns.

How benevolent are thy designs, O lord of eternity!
There is a Nile in the sky for strangers
And for the antelopes of all the highlands that go about upon
their feet.
But the Nile, it cometh from the Nether World for Egypt.

*The Seasons*

Thy rays nourish every garden;
When thou risest they live,
They grow by thee.
Thou makest the seasons
In order to make develop all that thou hast made.
Winter to bring them coolness,
And heat that they may taste thee.

*Universal Dominion*

Thou didst make the distant sky in order to rise therein,
In order to behold all that thou hast made,
While thou wast yet alone
Shining in thy form as living Aton,
Dawning, glittering, going afar and returning.
Thou makest millions of forms
Through thyself alone;
Cities, villages and fields, highways and rivers.
All eyes see thee before them,
For thou art Aton of the day over the earth.
When thou hast gone away,
And all men, whose faces thou hast fashioned

In order that thou mightest no longer see thyself alone,
Have fallen asleep, so that not one seeth that which thou hast
made,
Yet art thou still in my heart.

*Revelation to the King*

. . . . . . . . . . . . . . . . . . . . . . . . . . . . . . . . . . . . . . . .

There is no other that knoweth thee
Save thy son Ikhnaton.
Thou hast made him wise
In thy designs and in thy might.

*Universal Maintenance*

The world subsists in thy hand,
Even as thou hast made them.
When thou hast risen they live,
When thou settest they die;
For thou art length of life of thyself,
Men live through thee.

The eyes of men see beauty
Until thou settest.
All labour is put away
When thou settest in the west.
When thou risest again
Thou makest every hand to flourish for the king
And prosperity is in every foot,
Since thou didst establish the world,
And raise them up for thy son,
Who came forth from thy flesh,
The king of Upper and Lower Egypt,
Living in Truth, Lord of Two Lands,
Nefer-khepru-Re, Wan-Re (Ikhnaton),
Son of Re, living in Truth, lord of diadems,
Ikhnaton, whose life is long;
(And for) the chief royal wife, his beloved,
Mistress of the Two Lands, Nefer-nefru-Aton, Nofretete,
Living and flourishing for ever and ever.

Since both king and queen are mentioned by name in the introduction to the hymn, we might infer that Nefertiti shared in its authorship. On the other hand, such a salutation may have been a ritualistic usage implying nothing as to authorship.

The modern reader is amazed to discover that words of this nature were composed in the fourteenth century B.C. He is lost in admiration for the genius who could give expression to such lofty sentiment in this early period. Judged either as poetry or as theology, the hymn deserves a prominent place in any anthology of religious literature. One must acknowledge that it is far more inspiring than the imprecatory language of some of the psalms found in the "responsive readings" of the Christian ritual. For the first time in history, God was conceived as the father of all mankind. Not for many centuries, if at all, were any other such purely monotheistic teachings composed. Only in the writing of Deutero-Isaiah (sixth century B.C.) can we discern anything that approaches the universalism of Ikhnaton, and even then the teaching is quite fragmentary. Saint Francis' "Hymn to the Sun" (twelfth century A.D.), with its reverence for nature, is strikingly reminiscent of Ikhnaton's hymn. Still later we hear echoes of it in the poems of Wordsworth and most profoundly in Addison's hymn:

> The spacious firmament on high,
> With all the blue ethereal sky,
> And spangled heavens, a shining frame,
> Their great Original proclaim.
> Th'unwearied sun from day to day
> Does his Creator's power display,
> And publishes to every land
> The work of an almighty hand.

Attention has been called many times to the resemblance of the 104th psalm of the Old Testament to Ikhnaton's hymn. The following parallels illustrate the similarities:

*The Aton Hymn*

When thou settest in the western horizon of the sky,
The earth is in darkness like death.

Every lion cometh forth from his den,
All serpents, they sting.
Darkness broods,
The world is in silence,
He that made them resteth in his horizon.

Bright is the earth when thou risest in the horizon;
When thou shinest as Aton by day
Thou drivest away the darkness.
When thou sendest forth thy rays,
The Two Lands are in daily festivity.

The barques sail upstream and downstream alike.
Every highway is open because thou dawnest.
The fish in the river leap up before thee.
Thy rays are in the midst of the great green sea.

*104th Psalm*

Thou makest darkness, and it is night,
Wherein all the beasts of the forest creep forth.

The young lions roar after their prey,
And seek their food from God.

The sun ariseth, they get them away,
And lay them down in their dens.
Man goeth forth unto his work
And to his labour until the evening.

Yonder is the sea, great and wide,
Wherein are things creeping innumerable,
Both small and great beasts.
There go the ships;
There is leviathan, whom thou hast formed to play therein.

Similarity, of course, does not always imply dependence, and the question of the influence of the Egyptian hymn upon the Hebrew psalmist is more or less academic. In view of what happened to Akhetaton immediately after the death of the king, it is unlikely that the Hebrews knew anything about Ikhnaton's religion.

There is the bare possibility, as Breasted suggests, that some emissary of Ikhnaton may have taken the hymn to Palestine, where it became known by the later Hebrews. It is more likely, however, that some of the lines of the hymns survived the revolution and were applied in the Nineteenth Dynasty to Amon, in which case transmission to other countries would have been more probable.

The possibility that the monotheism of Moses (1200 B.C.) was influenced by Atonism is even more remote. The religion of Moses was far from monotheistic. Other gods were worshiped by the Hebrews for several centuries after the time of Moses. Yahweh was at best a tribal deity, interested only in his pact with Israel, a god of wrath and vengeance, with little resemblance to Aton. Furthermore, there is little likelihood that Atonism was transmitted to the Hebrews, even though there may have been Hebrew slaves in Egypt in the Amarna Age. Atonism remained exclusively the religion of Ikhnaton and his retinue, and disappeared with the destruction of Akhetaton, although it may have appeared briefly in Heliopolis during and after the Amarna period. The true Hebrew monotheism of the sixth and fifth centuries B.C. was the result of a long cultural growth in the land of Canaan and in the Babylonian Exile. The Hebrew theism was for the most part an indigenous achievement.

The second and shorter hymn is perhaps less encompassing than the longer one; but it is no less eloquent in its praise of Aton as beneficent creator.

*The Shorter Hymn*

Thou risest beautifully, O living Aton, Lord of Eternity;
Thou art glittering, beautiful, strong;
Thy love is great and mighty,
Thy rays furnish vision to every one of thy creatures,
Thy glowing hue brings life to the hearts of men,
When thou hast filled the Two Lands with thy love.
O God, who himself fashioned himself,
Maker of every land,
Creator of that which is upon it:
Even men, all herds of cattle and the antelopes,
All trees that grow in the soil,
They live when thou dawnest for them,
Thou art the mother and the father of all that thou hast made.
As for their eyes, when thou dawnest,
They see by means of thee.
Thy rays illuminate the whole earth,
And every heart rejoices because of seeing thee,
When thou dawnest as their lord.

When thou settest in the western horizon of the sky,
They sleep after the manner of the dead,
Their heads are wrapped up,
Their nostrils are stopped,
Until thy rising comes in the morning,
In the eastern horizon of the sky.
Then their arms are uplifted in adoration of thee,
Thou makest the hearts of men to live by thy beauty,
For men live when thou sendest forth thy rays,
Every land is in festivity:
Singing, music, and shouting of joy
Are in the hall of the Benben-house,
Thy temple in Akhetaton, the seat of Truth,
Wherewith thou art satisfied.
Food and provision are offered therein;
Thy pure son performs thy pleasing ceremonies,
O living Aton, at his festal processions.

All that thou hast made dance before thee,
Thy august son rejoices, his heart is joyous,
O living Aton, born in the sky every day.
He begets his august son Wan-re (Ikhnaton)
Like himself without ceasing,
Son of Re, wearing his beauty, Nefer-khepru-Re, Wan-Re
(Ikhnaton),
Even me, thy son, in whom thou art satisfied,
Who bears thy name.
Thy strength and thy might abide in my heart,
Even thine, O Aton, living forever . . .
Thou hast made the distant sky to rise therein,
In order to behold all that thou didst make,
While thou wast yet alone.
Myriads of life are in thee to sustain them alive,
For it is the breath of life in the nostrils to behold thy radiance.
All flowers live and what grows in the soil
Is made to grow because thou dawnest.
They are drunken before thee.
All cattle skip upon their feet;
The birds in the marsh fly with joy,
Their wings that were folded are spread,
Uplifted in adoration to the living Aton,
Thou maker . . .

The faith of Ikhnaton, as revealed in these hymns, contained many qualities usually attributed to later thinkers. One is the concept of constraining love. Aton binds all people and all nations together in his tender love. A second " modern " idea is Ikhnaton's doctrine of immanence. Although Aton is transcendent, his power pervades all life on the earth.

Though thou art far away,
Thy rays are upon the earth;
Though thou art on high,
Thy footprints are the day.

The idea of the god bestowing his blessings upon his creatures is most graphically represented in the Amarna paintings and reliefs which portray the solar disc, from which long rays descend terminating in human hands which hold the Ankh, or sign of life. Such a symbol suggests the power of deity in the affairs of men through the life-giving rays of the disc. Here we note one of the most distinctive features of Ikhnaton's religion. In every Amarna relief, the rays are given the most prominent place as the source of radiant energy. In so picturing the deity, Ikhnaton broke from the anthropomorphic, as well as from the totally transcendent conception of deity, to formulate the more profound idea of God's immanence. For the first time in history, God was conceived as a formless being. The God of Genesis walked about " in the garden in the cool of the day " and talked to Adam and Eve. The Yahweh of Moses was a god of wrath and vengeance. Ikhnaton's god was the Lord of Peace, an intangible essence, the energetic force that acted through the sun, the creator who held all things in his hands. It was hundreds of years before any thinker again referred to God as compassionate, merciful and tender — a beneficent creator, loving all creatures, great and small.

One of the most conspicuous elements in the religion of Ikhnaton is the joy of life, the sheer delight in God's creation. Here was a poet finding God in the contemplation of nature, in the enjoyment of sunshine, and in the simple life. God is the loving Father who caused the birds to flutter in their marshes, the sheep to dance in the fields and the fish to leap in the river. Such a naive appreciation of nature — if one may use the expression — has characterized all creative periods in history — the Golden Age of Greece, the Italian Renaissance, the Romantic Era in England and the Concord Period in American letters. The feeling of ecstasy and rapture in being a part of life, the *joie de vivre* so prominent in these hymns, recalls a line of Browning: " How good is man's life, the mere living! "

A final noteworthy aspect is that God was thought to be the sole creator. " While he was still alone " Aton created all things and his creativity was everlasting. " Thou makest millions of forms through thyself alone." With surprising sensitivity and almost childlike wonder, the God-intoxicated prophet wonders at the creative capacity of Aton in calling forth life even from such a small thing as an egg.

> When the fledgling in the egg chirps in the shell,
> Thou givest him breath therein to preserve him alive.

The joy of being alive pervades the picture of the chick emerging from the shell and chirping with delight:

> He cometh forth from the egg
> To chirp with all his might.
> He goeth about upon his two feet
> When he hath come forth therefrom.

Ikhnaton taught not only the universality of God but his eternal duration. Aton, the author of his own being, was " the reminder of eternity," without beginning or end. This thought is reminiscent of Spinoza's idea of God as " creative nature existing in infinite attributes and endless time."

The Egyptian's traditional exaltation of the Nile as a source of life has already been discussed. The river was identified with Osiris, the god of life and immortality. The heresy of Ikhnaton's religion is more apparent when we perceive his total rejection of the deification of the Nile as identified with Osiris. Ignoring all mythological traditions, he attributes the annual overflow to natural forces created by Aton — an unmistakable expression of the naturalistic or rational point of view. Osiris, in fact, is not mentioned anywhere in the Amarna literature. But while Ikhnaton sees the phenomenon of the Nile's inundation as natural, he goes beyond the materialistic explanation to the ultimate divine source. In fact, his conception of God as the author of the universe, omnipresent and immanent, revealing himself in the visible world, was not only an iconoclastic idea for his day, but it also anticipated much of what usually goes under the name of modern religious philosophy. The philosopher-king addressed his God as " the father and mother of all that thou hast made." To him the earth was " filled with the glory of God." All living creatures rejoiced in the beauty of the earth and exulted in the radiant presence of God.

> All creatures that fly or alight,
> They live when thou hast shone upon them.

The presence of God was identified with light itself. Even after Aton had " gone to rest in the horizon," he was present in the hearts of men.

Ikhnaton's ecstatic exaltation of light may be compared to the feelings of Ruskin in his contemplation of " the breathing, animated exulting light, which feels and receives and rejoices and acts . . . leaping from rock to rock, from leaf to leaf, from wave to wave. It is the living light which sleeps but never dies." In this teaching of the beneficence of the natural order and sheer delight in its manifestations, we discern an anticipation of the nineteenth century " return-to-nature " movement.

Such was the genius of Ikhnaton's religious reform. It is not enough to say that it was materialistic. His ecstatic delight in the earth as a manifestation of God's benevolent and continued presence is an expression of spiritual monism unsurpassed in religious literature.

Much has been made of the absence of ethics in the

religion of Amarna. Admittedly the two hymns contain no explicit teaching about righteousness or integrity, but the argument of silence is never conclusive. Furthermore, the surviving literature is only fragmentary and there may well have been other documents more directly concerned with morality. The solar theology of Heliopolis was concerned with moral values and, dependent as it was on the religion of Ra, it is hard to understand why Atonism should have neglected the earlier emphasis on ethics. It is improbable that the two hymns found on the walls of the nobles' tombs constitute Ikhnaton's entire system of thought. Repeated references to the " teaching " of Ikhnaton found in the tombs indicate that he had composed some formal doctrine which was later destroyed by his enemies. He must have subscribed to the earlier ethical principles of the Heliopolitan solar faith, for his use of the phrase " Living in Truth " in all official documents bearing his name clearly implies that he followed the doctrine of *maat*.

Regardless of the presence or absence of moral values in the surviving literature, the fact is that Ikhnaton's actions were those of a person with a high moral standard of living. He was convinced that hatred, conquest and war were inconsistent with the universal love of God, and he acted on that belief. If God has good will toward all men, it must follow that his children should have good will toward each other. This meant outright pacifism, a pacifism to which he adhered even though it ultimately meant his political ruin.

The two hymns, together with whatever other inscriptions remained, testify to the king's personal integrity and devotion to truth. The following statements, for example, appear in the tomb of Ay: " The king put truth in my body and my abomination is lying. I know that Ikhnaton rejoices in the truth." The sun-god is one whose " heart is satisfied with truth, whose abomination is falsehood."

The reform of Ikhnaton has been relegated to a purely political category by several historians. This ignores the impact of these two great hymns of universalism. There is something fresh and original in them, a new spirit, something with a sweep that had never been known before. Here was a genius who anticipated the " one world, one god " idea of our own day. God is the creator of the natural world and all that is in it. God's beneficence includes all peoples regardless of race or clime. True, Ikhnaton's conception of God, as far as we know, does not contain the quality of righteousness so characteristic of the Hebrew prophets; but his is the God of truth and integrity, principles which the king applied in both public and private life.

It is also clear that the religion of Amarna contained no relics of the old sacerdotalism, with its magic and charms. Gone were the *ushabti* figures, the scarabs and all mechanical instruments of salvation. Banished were the superstitions of the Osirian faith, gods and demigods and traditional ceremonies. Here were no graven images, for the god Aton was without form. Here was no mention of hatred, jealousy or wrath, of hell or of the judgment of God, for Aton was tender and compassionate. It was the first time in history that such qualities were attributed to God. For that matter, nowhere had deity ever been conceived of as one spiritual entity.

It is precisely at this point that we can appreciate the greatness of the young king. Conventional belief and age-long custom rule the minds of people in any era, but this was especially true of ancient Egypt, where the slightest departure from tradition was anathema and the validity of an idea lay in its conformity to the past. In Ikhnaton we have an individual who swept tradition aside, discarded all polytheistic myths and abolished all ancient rites, however sacrosanct. In their place, he appealed simply to the clear and natural manifestations of God " in whom we live, move and have our being," as a later prophet wrote. This profound simplicity, the product of one man's mind, is the key to Ikhnaton's genius and justifies his high place as the first in the line of the prophets.

# VII Living in Truth

One of the most charming pieces of art to be recovered from the Amarna ruins is a colored relief which pictures Ikhnaton and Nefertiti facing each other in an informal pose. Casually leaning on his staff, the king talks to his wife, who half teasingly holds a small bouquet of flowers to his nose for him to smell. In the other hand she holds a bouquet of lotus flowers. Her gown is ruffled by the breeze, as is the king's hair. The simplicity of this relief aptly illustrates the way in which the heresy of Ikhnaton expressed itself in the art and family life of the palace. The philosophy of naturalism so clearly seen in both the religion and art of Amarna is epitomized in the king's motto or guiding principle, " Living in Truth."

The often recurring word *maat,* or truth, has given rise to much discussion among Egyptologists. We have called attention earlier to the essential meaning of the term which refers to the cosmic order, the rightness of things in the world of nature, as well as to justice and truth in human life. It stood for permanence and immutability as personified in the king. This sense of permanence, order and stability was re-enforced by the artistic representation of royalty. The god-king, guardian of *maat,* was always sculptured in a rigid, immobile form, majestic and unchanging.

The apparent contradiction between Ikhnaton's use of *maat,* on one hand, and his violation of the sacred canons of art, on the other, can be reconciled only if one assumes he used the word to imply fidelity to the natural world and to human life, the depiction of nature and the human form faithfully and in accordance with life as one finds it; hence, the realism in the portrait of himself and his wife as well as in the paintings of animal and bird life. The revolution in art was in fact an application of *maat*, " truthfulness." This naturalness had already appeared to a certain extent in the reign of Amenhotep III. Like the shift from the stylized art of the Middle Ages to the naturalism of the Renaissance, it was a change from the otherworldly to the secular.

In the light of the long history of conventional Egyptian art, the Amarna period might well be called abnormal. Although some distortion is present, art in Ikhnaton's time was essentially a portrayal of things as they were. Egyptian art both before and after the period was a representation of things according to their importance in the traditional Egyptian cosmology.

As applied to art Ikhnaton's motto, *maat*, meant a clean break with the stereotyped forms of the Egyptian tradition and the projection of a new dynamic naturalism which portrayed life as it actually was. All previous representations of royalty showed the king seated with unbending dignity and august immobility, or, if standing, with the left leg advanced, arms hung straight at the sides, fists clenched and head facing straight ahead. Ikhnaton thrust aside convention and trained his artists in a new realistic style which depicted human beings as they really looked. The king is always pictured with his family, even at state functions such as the occasion of rewarding the high priest with gifts or bestowing collars of gold upon faithful courtiers. In one tomb painting, he and his wife lean over the cushioned balcony of the Window of Appearances to confer honors upon the priest, Ay, and his wife, while the little

*Photograph by Walter Steinkopf, Berlin-Dahlem.*
*Berlin Museum.*

Nefertiti offering Ikhnaton flowers. Painted limestone relief. The casual pose of the king, leaning on his staff, and the pert expression of the queen, holding the flowers for her husband to smell, illustrate vividly the realism of Amarna.

princesses bring more golden collars to their parents for presentation. In the background, dancers and musicians entertain and boys dance for joy. The waiting chariots of the priests are above. Scribes carefully record the event, making note of the gifts presented. In another tomb picture of the royal couple riding in a chariot, the queen is kissing the king while a princess leans over the front of the chariot, goading the horses with a stick.

One of the most unconventional scenes is found on a relief in the tomb of Huya. The royal family is celebrating the arrival in Amarna of the queen mother. Tiy, wearing the royal headdress, sits facing the king and queen. Ikhnaton is eating what appears to be a skewer of charcoal-broiled *shish kebab,* while his lady, wearing only a simple skirt or apron, holds a whole roast duck in her hands. The queen mother is trying to decide whether to choose something from the heavily laden table of food before her or to take one of the cakes offered her by the young princess at her feet. Two large tables covered with plates of food stand before the king and queen. The other four children sit on the floor amusing themselves with games. Another relief from the same tomb shows the continuation of the celebration a few hours later when all are drinking wine. One princess stands on a footstool with a glass of wine in her hand while another, unnoticed by the rest, snatches some cookies. In these scenes the royal pair is often seen sitting together with their arms around each other and in one relief the queen is seated on the king's knee. These uninhibited scenes are typical of the Amarna reliefs, but it is a far cry from anything before or since in Egyptian art.

A very noticeable aspect of the Amarna revolution was Ikhnaton's rejection of all the traditional court etiquette and convention which made the life of the king a continual

*Photograph, courtesy The Metropolitan Museum of Art*

Seated statue of Amenemhet III (1840–1790 B.C.), in the Cairo Museum. Wearing *nemes* headdress with serpent and pendant, and illustrating conventional pose of kings in statuary. From Hawara.

385.

round of artificial poses and gestures. Rather than holding himself aloof from the people, Ikhnaton lived among them. When he rode through the city or appeared at public ceremonies he was always accompanied by his wife and children. In the work of artists we see wonderfully preserved the expression of his intense love of naturalness and simplicity, and his belief in the sanctity and beauty of the family.

The king was intent upon teaching his followers of the dignity and beauty of family life, for he took pains to have his artists portray the most intimate scenes of palace life: the royal family relaxing over some food or wine; the king and queen engaging in conversation, with the children playing about the room; and other such informal occasions. But such scenes are not limited to the privacy of the palace. While riding upon the royal palanquin, the queen holds her arm around the king's waist and rests her head on his shoulder. The king is seen kissing his wife as he drives his chariot through the streets of Akhetaton. The utter realism of these domestic representations suggests that even the king's private life was ruled by the motto "Living in Truth." He loved his queen and was not ashamed for the world to know it. His affection for her was the truth, and he proclaimed such a happy family life to be the true way of living. This sincere and unaffected display of affection is a unique thing in the art of ancient Egypt, with its stilted sphinx-like poses. The king's tender feeling toward his wife is further displayed in many royal inscriptions, where he refers to her as "Mistress of the King's happiness," "Chief Wife of the King beloved by him," "The Lady of Grace" and "Fair of Countenance." Such expressions were usually not consistent with the austerity of the court, or at least were not taken seriously; but in the case of Ikhnaton and Nefertiti, there can be no doubt of genuineness. The

*Photograph by Walter Steinkopf, Berlin-Dahlem. Berlin Museum*

Ikhnaton, Nefertiti and their children. A limestone relief from the royal palace at Tell el-Amarna. Under the radiating arms of Aton the king and queen are seated, holding the royal princesses. The king is seen kissing his daughter.

queen gave no son to Ikhnaton, but there is no evidence that he paid any attention to any of his secondary wives. Contrary to Egyptian custom, he apparently remained strictly monogamous.

That Ikhnaton's principle of "Living in Truth" guided his painters and sculptors is clear from the character of their work, especially that of Thutmose, the king's chief sculptor. Thutmose worked from both the living model and from life masks. With this method, he created the brown sandstone head and exquisite limestone bust of Queen Nefertiti, considered to be one of the great masterpieces of sculpture.

In the magnificent head the sculptor has captured a poignancy and pensiveness of facial expression and an air of grace unexcelled in the history of art. Such a face clearly belonged to a most gracious and sympathetic personality. Nefertiti impresses one as being completely modern. The details of this life-sized bust are so unbelievably real that it seems to come alive before one's eyes. It is carved from soft limestone and painted in blue, red, yellow, green, white, black and flesh color.

It is nothing short of miraculous that this fragile statue should be found practically intact, after having been buried for nearly thirty-three hundred years. It is in perfect condition, except for some slight damage to the headdress and ears and the absence of one eye. The right eye is made of rock crystal and the pupil of brownish wood. The absence of the left eye has provoked considerable discussion among archaeologists. Had Nefertiti suffered from an opthalmic ailment, so common in Egypt at that time, and actually lost her left eye? A thorough search in the debris surrounding the bust failed to produce the missing eye, although pieces of the ear were found. The head appears to have been made without the left eye. On the other hand,

*Photograph by Walter Steinkopf, Berlin-Dahlem. Berlin Museum.*

Portrait bust of Nefertiti from Tell el-Amarna. Painted limestone. The queen wears a blue headdress with a band and uraeus. This bust was found in the workshop of the chief sculptor, Thutmose, by Ludwig Borchardt. Right eye unfinished.

other busts of the queen done by the same artist show no such defect. It is possible, therefore, that the present head was never completed. Another suggestion has been made that Thutmose had fallen in love with the queen but that it was an unreciprocated love. Some time after the head was completed, Nefertiti contracted an eye disease. Thutmose then removed the eye from the statue and inserted a white stone in the socket, preferring not to see her as she once was.

Another question is posed by the fact that along with the almost perfectly preserved statue of the queen the archaeologists found a shattered statue of her husband. Why was the one destroyed and the other left untouched? After Ikhnaton's death and the removal of the court to Thebes, Nefertiti moved to the northern extremity of Akhetaton. The two busts were probably left by Thutmose on a shelf in his studio. The most logical explanation is that when the reactionaries from Thebes destroyed the city of Akhetaton they threw the king's statue to the floor and broke it into fragments, but had no particular reason for mutilating the statue of the queen. Perhaps it fell to the floor later, when the shelf deteriorated, injuring the ears and head slightly.

There is still greater mystery surrounding the subsequent history of the bust of Nefertiti. It was in 1912 that the German expedition, under Ludwig Borchardt, came upon the famous statue of the queen in Thutmose's studio. Arrangements for digging in Egypt by foreign expeditions were made through the Egyptian Department of Antiquities. At the conclusion of the season's digging, it was customary for the head archaeologist to report to the director-general of the Egyptian Antiquities Service. After inspecting the objects found, the director decided what should remain in the Cairo Museum and what could be taken away by the visiting archaeologists. Usually, in Iraq and Egypt, the objects have been divided equally except where an intact Egyptian royal tomb was discovered, in which case all the contents remained in Cairo – the only instance of this circumstance being the discovery of the tomb of Tutankhamon.

In line with this procedure, Pierre Lacau, the French director of the Egyptian Antiquities Service, was asked to go to Tell el-Amarna to inspect the objects on display. The German archaeologists told him that there was nothing of any great consequence but that they were interested in sending the material to Berlin for study. So Lacau sent a young assistant whose inspection revealed nothing but several baskets of broken pottery and many scattered fragments of sandstone. Satisfied that there was nothing that was vital to the Cairo Museum, the young inspector signed the papers permitting the material to be shipped out of the country.

Nothing was heard of the shipment until 1925, when the announcement appeared of the " recent acquisition " to the Berlin Museum of the exquisite bust of Nefertiti. The Egyptian authorities naturally wanted to know when and how this statue was acquired. For a while no explanation was forthcoming, but finally the Germans confessed that they had found the bust during their 1912–1914 expedition and that it had been awarded them by the director of Antiquities in the division of excavated objects. When it was confirmed that the French assistant at Cairo had seen and approved only some broken fragments of stone, the Berlin authorities explained that they were not aware of the identity of the bust or of its importance until the pieces had been put together in the Berlin Museum.

Upon receiving this implausible explanation, the Egyptian government, convinced that they had been duped and that the bust, intact or otherwise, had not gone through the inspection at Amarna, requested its return to Egypt. The request was promptly refused. After several more unsuccessful attempts to negotiate with Berlin, the Egyptian authorities sent word that until the celebrated statue was returned to its rightful owners no further German archaeological expeditions in Egypt would be permitted. The queen was kept in Berlin, and no German excavations have been conducted in Egypt since 1914.

The controversy over Nefertiti brought about a change in the regulations governing foreign archaeological projects in Egypt. Previously, permission to excavate had been granted to individuals as well as to museums, and a fair division of the findings was made under the supervision of the director-general. In 1924 this rule was rescinded and it was announced that henceforth foreign expeditions could not expect to take out any of the objects found except in the case of duplicates, a regulation that proved unsatisfactory to most museums.

During World War II the bust of Nefertiti disappeared from the State Museum of Berlin. In 1945 it was recovered by a United States Army Team from a salt mine where it had been hidden for safekeeping, tenderly wrapped in glass wool. It was then placed with other valuable objects in the Wiesbaden Central Collecting Point, where it remained on exhibition under the eye of the United States government. Soon after, her gracious majesty, the queen, was restored to her throne in the Berlin Museum where she now presides over her world court.

The close association of the king with his artists is plainly evident in a tablet which refers to the royal architect, Bek, as " the assistant whom his Majesty himself taught, chief of sculptors on the great and mighty monuments of the king." This inscription does not necessarily imply that Ikhnaton instructed his artists in the technical detail, but rather in the application of his principle "Living in Truth." The unprecedented realism of Amarna reliefs, some of which we have tried to describe, shows how thoroughly the artists were indoctrinated. Within the framework of that principle, they were undoubtedly free to portray things as they saw them, untrammeled by the dictates of hallowed tradition and court propriety. The revolution in art effected by the Amarna School influenced greatly the technique of human portraiture. Plant and animal life, marsh and river scenes had been portrayed in a fairly realistic manner in previous periods, so that the artists of Akhetaton were only continuing and accentuating that trend. The Amarna artists were unique, however, in their representations of the human figure. They depicted the daily events of life in a sincere and honest way. They pictured the king and his family unaffectedly enjoying the simple pleasures of domestic life. They modeled the human figure so realistically that one might think that some of their sculptures, such as the torso of one of the princesses, came from fifth-century Athens.

It would seem, in fact, that Ikhnaton's artists carried this realism almost to the point of caricature, particularly in picturing the king with a distinctly distended stomach. Some authorities feel that the king was afflicted with a disease which was characterized by the overdevelopment of the head, lips and lower part of the body. These peculiarities are shown in practically all of the Amarna reliefs and sculptures. If the king had such abnormalities, he may well have insisted on being depicted in this realistic manner. But his artists did not stop there. They began to exaggerate the abnormality and even pictured Nefertiti and the children in the same way. The habit seems to have become a fad, for later the priests and nobles were similarly drawn. Fragments of two colossal statues of Ikhnaton, which are now in Berlin, show a complete departure from the natural or realistic form. They are fantastic caricatures, with long and emaciated faces, high cheekbones, slit, almost closed eyes, large ears, long beard, thin arms and enlarged stomach. Such a grotesque style seems to represent an *art nouveau* or ancient school of expressionism. Some of the reliefs of the period pursue their baroque mannerisms still further. But this insistence ultimately caused the undoing of the Amarna School, for after Ikhnaton's death, artists completely rejected the realistic style and conscientiously returned to orthodoxy. Consequently, the normal continuity of artistic expression was lost, and the unique contribution of this period was not absorbed into the historic streams of Egyptian art except in the Nineteenth Dynasty, where certain traces of Amarna influence can be detected.

As we have already indicated, realism had not been entirely lacking in earlier Egyptian art, but before the Amarna period it played only a minor role. Traditional Egyptian painting or sculpture was primarily ideoplastic; that is, the form was used to symbolize an idea rather than a fact and was therefore conceptual in its aim rather than photographic. Thus, where the artistic expression was primarily ideological, realism could be only a subordinate factor and the work frequently lacked specific detail. The originality of the art of Amarna lay in its photographic accuracy, in its aim to present an actual likeness rather than an ideological symbol.

This new philosophy of art produced a significant change. Now, instead of applying a conventional form to a particular subject and adding a minimum of new detail, the artist introduced a psychological element by portraying the subject in a unique or particular situation, with bodily posture and facial expression giving the sensation of an

*Cairo Museum*

Colossal sandstone statue of Ikhnaton. From the Aton Temple in Karnak. Although sculptured before the reform and departure from Thebes, the exaggerated qualities of the later Amarna sculpture are noticeable here also. The name of Amon was erased from all statues but this in the new kingdom.

actual happening rather than producing a conventionalized pattern. In other words, the Amarna School depicted actual scenes from life and not abstract ideas. One tomb relief, for instance, pictures Mahu, chief of police at Amarna, receiving messengers. Nearby a brazier, with brightly burning coals, suggests that it is a chilly day. Such a touch of particularity shows the new realistic style.

Furthermore, the action of each picture is placed in its original setting — a palace, a field or a house — giving greater realism by providing the appropriate landscape or background. This does not imply perspective in the modern sense of the word, but it is an advance over all previous art.

Another " modern " characteristic of the work of Ikhnaton's artists is the unity of composition. The gestures or facial expressions of the various figures in a group combine to concentrate the viewer's attention on one central point. All the figures are related and are presented in a unified whole. Even in wall paintings, each section constitutes a unified scene with an important figure in the center and subsidiary figures at the sides; formerly, such decorative murals were mechanically arranged in a series of disconnected scenes.

The murals of Amarna — found in the palaces, in the houses of the nobles and in the rock tombs — exist only in fragments, but enough remains to provide abundant evidence of the artists' complete absorption in the production of realistic representations rather than conceptual images.

The Green Room of the North Palace had large unbroken wall surfaces which were covered with one continuous picture, giving the appearance of wallpaper, except that there was no repetition of motif. The scene pictured is a marsh containing graceful papyrus plants. Lotus blossoms and green leaves float on the blue water. The bank is covered with grasses and weeds which bend under the weight of their buds. The thicket teems with life: rock pigeons and palm doves, small birds nesting with their young, the pied shrike and the black and white kingfisher. The diving kingfisher is just about to hit the water — an excellent example of Amarna realism. There is nothing original in marsh scenes with bird life and decorative borders, but the walls of the Green Room show a creativeness and freedom never before displayed in Egyptian art. Previously a papyrus thicket was shown only as a setting for a hunting expedition. Here is nature for nature's sake, a restful scene unmolested by the destructive activities of man.

The tombs of the Amarna officials, Nakht and Ramose, provide further evidence of the revolution in art under Ikhnaton. Nakht, a priest of Amon, has served the young king at Thebes and later accompanied him to the new city as a priest of Aton. A mural in his tomb shows an informal domestic scene of the priest and his wife at dinner. An attendant serves them geese and grapes. A son arranges flowers. Several guests, seated nearby, are engaged in conversation, and a harpist plays. A cat is eating fish. Another relief shows an agricultural scene: Nakht overseeing laborers who are plowing and sowing seed. Some are breaking up the hard earth, while others fell trees. Other scenes portray the farming process right up to the reaping and winnowing and measuring of the grain.

The funeral scene in the tomb of Ramose in Thebes (where he returned after Nakht had succeeded him as Ikhnaton's vizier) is one of the most striking paintings ever found in Egypt. In this scene, the body of the vizier is being borne into the tomb on the heads of the bearers, who are preceded and followed by attendants carrying funerary

*Cairo Museum*

Funeral scene, painting on limestone, in tomb of Ramose in Thebes; one of the most dramatic and realistic relief scenes in Egypt. Most striking are the tears on the faces of the mourning women.

equipment. Facing the procession is a group of mourners whose posture and expression of grief are most vividly portrayed. Also in the tomb of Ramose is a relief of the king receiving foreign ambassadors. Here again, the artist has concentrated on the exaggerated features of the king — his long face, prominent lips and chin. The bas-relief portraits of Ramose and his wife are delicately carved and, fortunately, well preserved. They are well known for their elaborate wigs and the detailed sculpturing of the faces.

As we have suggested, the new spirit of Amarna was something like that of the Renaissance in Italy and later in Holland, when artists, thrilling to the new freedom and candid recognition of the natural world, painted real people living their daily lives; kitchens and barnyards; the action of the moment, not the eternal pose. Ikhnaton's artists were likewise concerned with motion, actuality, individuality, action. This is illustrated in the Window-of-the-Appearances scenes, where the traditionally pompous presentation of gifts here becomes extremely informal. The king tosses the golden collars to his favorites and the spectators unashamedly join in the festivities. Excitement and hilarity dominate the scene.

The decorative needs of the city — and there were many — demanded a considerable glass and faience industry. Excavations show the remains of two large glazing plants and several glass factories. Judging from the waste-piles of the shops and the surviving examples of colored glazes and glass in the houses of the nobles, the temples, tombs and palaces, these factories were constantly busy during the few years that the city was in existence. Glaze had been used in Egypt from the earliest period, but its manufacture reached its artistic peak at Amarna, as the vases of turquoise and lapis lazuli blue now in the various collections of the world testify. The palm leaf capitals of

*Courtesy R. B. Fleming & Co. Ltd., London*

A section of the " Kingfisher and Doves " painting in the Green Room of the North Palace at Amarna (illustration, page 154 also).

the palace columns were perhaps the most lavish examples of the use of colored glazes and gold inlay. Precious stones were set within gold lines like cloisonné around the top of the columns, creating the most brilliant effect imaginable.

All of the innovations produced in the Amarna period are to be seen, of course, as an integral part of the great reform of Ikhnaton and the expression of his principle, " Living in Truth." We have seen the application of this in the open candor of his family life, the naturalism in art and the free and open worship of the spirit of the sun. With Ikhnaton truth came first. In art, truth meant fidelity to visual observation, not stylized portrayal of a philosophical principle. The superficiality of this realism accounts for its disappearance after the death of the king.

There is reason to believe that the art of the late Eighteenth Dynasty was influenced by Crete. It was during the reign of Amenhotep III that the Minoan empire came to a catastrophic end with the sack of Knossos, and some historians conclude that many artists and craftsmen fled to Egypt and that the new spirit in Egyptian art was due in part to Minoan influence. There is a similarity between the two in the desire for a more personal, realistic, less abstract motif. Perhaps the revolutionary realism of Ikhnaton's art received its initial impetus from Crete. Be that as it may, the Amarna movement in art cannot be dissociated from the king himself.

*Courtesy R. B. Fleming & Co. Ltd., London*

The kingfisher in Green Room painting is shown in the act of diving into the water — an excellent example of Amarna realism in art.

# VIII The Curse of Amon

Throughout his reign, Ikhnaton's Foreign Office was a busy place. Messengers from foreign cities arrived almost daily with reports, some of which we have previously quoted. Palestinian and Syrian kings urgently requested aid against the Hittites, who now presented the greatest threat to the empire. Aziru, the Egyptian vassal in charge of an Amorite kingdom, along with two other kings, co-operated with the Hittites in their seizure of northern Syria. Ikhnaton was informed of this loss and was warned of further invasion. Rib-addi, the ruler of Byblos in Phoenicia, wrote repeatedly to the pharaoh for help and Abi-milki of Tyre asked for troops.

While Aziru was slaying Egyptian officials in Syria and taking their territory for the Amorites, he wrote Ikhnaton that he was busy helping to defend the Syrian cities against the Hittites and therefore could not appear at the court in Akhetaton, at least for a year. The king sent a reply granting him the year, but Aziru managed to avoid meeting the messenger and the letter was brought back to Egypt. Aziru then wrote regretting that his campaign against the Hittites in the north had prevented him from meeting the king's envoy.

Meanwhile appeals continued to come from Rib-addi for aid against Aziru. An Egyptian vassal in Galilee finally sent an expedition against Byblos and overcame the garrison. Rib-addi attempted to defend Byblos and the near-by coastal cities, but all fell to the enemy. He was finally slain, and with him went the northern part of the empire.

Palestine fared similarly under the invasion of the Habiri with the connivance of unfaithful vassals. Meggido, Askalon, Gezer and Lachish begged in vain for help. Ebed-hepa, the governor of Jerusalem, in one of his letters, added a personal note to Ikhnaton's cuneiform scribe, whom he apparently knew intimately: "To the scribe of my lord, the king. Ebed-hepa thy servant. Bring these words plainly before my lord, the king: 'The whole land of my lord, the king, is going to ruin.'" The Habiri swept over Palestine, burning the towns and driving the people out of the land.

Dispatches and special emissaries arrived constantly in the capital to impress upon the pharaoh the urgency of resistance, but the most Ikhnaton did was occasionally to dispatch a general with a small force, token gestures which proved to be totally ineffective. As in the case of the northern provinces, the Palestinian vassals were in league with the invaders, and misrepresented the situation in their reports to the king. Ebed-hepa was the only loyal representative in Palestine as Rib-addi was in Phoenicia.

In spite of the constant flow of letters and the frequent appearances of ambassadors at the court, the king and his counsellors did not appreciate the actual conditions. Most of Ikhnaton's viceroys had played into the hands of the enemy while suppressing the facts of the situation in their letters to him. At first glance it is inconceivable that the Egyptian authorities were actually so inept. Rib-addi's letters were crystal clear in their meaning and entirely obvious in their urgency. But it is also true that Rib-addi's enemies were also writing to Ikhnaton, professing the stoutest loyalty, and naming Rib-addi himself as the real traitor. While infiltrating the Phoenician cities and alienating them from Egypt, these Amorite scoundrels paid lip service to the king in their correspondence and prejudiced him against those who were faithful.

Perhaps the most Machiavellian of them all were 'Abdu-Ashirta, the Amorite chief, Aziru, his son, and Shubbiluliuma, the Hittite. The king did not act decisively in the crisis, but it must be remembered that all his information came from his Foreign Office. He received only what his ministers wished him to receive. It is known that Aziru, for instance, wrote all his letters directly to the king's chamberlain, who had charge of matters of state. With such censored reports Ikhnaton could not have known all the facts. The deception, misrepresentation and chaotic conditions abroad, plus the confusion at home, so clearly discernible in the Amarna letters, help us to understand the inaction of the king and his advisers.

Ikhnaton was no politician, and he was hopelessly lost in a sea of intrigue and lies. He lived in a world of truth, and naively believed that all other people did too. The fact is, of course, that his dominant interest was not in holding the empire, but in holding his kingdom of truth. In the earlier stages of disintegration in Asia, even a small show of force might have been enough to throw back the invaders and convince the enemy that Egypt was determined to hold her provinces, but having failed at that point, she was later powerless to stem the tide.

It was to be expected that sooner or later the loss of the Asiatic provinces and the failure of Ikhnaton to act in the crisis would have repercussions at Thebes. The wonder is that the once-powerful priesthood of Amon, together with the enraged military class, did not attempt to overthrow "the criminal of Akhetaton," as the king was now called by the Amon priests. As for the people at large, they were powerless, but it is safe to assume that there was much resentment toward the royal decree which had deprived them of their only means of spiritual security, their worship of Osiris, the god of the hereafter, and the magical formulae of the Book of the Dead. The Osirian faith, with its cultic paraphernalia, was something they could grasp; it gave them things to do that would assure them of salvation. But this new faith was abstract, and its god absolutely incomprehensible to them. The impact of the obliteration of the name of Amon was confined for the most part to Thebes, but the order to erase the names of all the gods of Egypt created consternation and discontent in other cities, where Ptah, Hathor and many other local deities were still worshiped. Both priests and populace throughout the country joined the Thebans in their revolt against this mad pharaoh. The common people could not worship a god who was so far removed and who had no visible representations.

Ikhnaton's last days must have been filled with disillusionment as he contemplated the future fate of Atonism after his death. It was too much to expect that Horemheb, Ay, Smenkhkara or Tutankhamon would be able to hold out against Thebes. Ikhnaton's peaceful policy would never be continued by those who longed for the restoration of the lost provinces and Egyptian power.

During the last two years of the reign, Queen Tiy probably brought pressure to bear on Ikhnaton. It is not unlikely that some of the provincial governors, receiving no replies from Ikhnaton, had appealed from time to time to Tiy at Thebes as well as to Horemheb. No doubt, these two had conferred long and often on the state of the nation. Tiy's state visits to Akhetaton were real pageants, but they did not signify any genuine interest in the new capital or its religion. Although she had supported the cause of Aton in its earlier phases, she had not favored the move to

Akhetaton. On these visits to Amarna the dowager queen must have urged Ikhnaton to act the part of a king and to leave the preaching to the priests. She probably tried to shame him into action by pointing out that while he and his friends were enjoying the peace of Aton in the dream city, his brothers in Syria and Palestine were being slain by the Hittite barbarians. While he isolated himself and his entourage in well-protected Akhetaton, which he had sworn never to leave, his tribute states were ravaged by invaders and betrayed by his own viceroys. How could he be content to praise Aton daily in the temple and sing of the joy of living when his subjects in Asia were facing death? Had he taken pains to learn the truth behind the letters from the treacherous Asiatic envoys? No! To the aging woman who had ruled the empire before it began to disintegrate, who had known the security bought by the conquests of her forebears and who had trained the young prince in the duties of an imperial kingship, the blind and fanatical isolationism of her son was more than she could tolerate.

Even more urgent were the visits of Horemheb to the court. He placed before the king the facts of the situation: the treachery of Aziru, the murder of Ikhnaton's loyal representatives and the march of the Hittites over Mitanni and Syria. Horemheb was the only adviser willing to risk offending the king by telling him the truth. He begged for the authority to take up arms against the aggressors before it was too late.

For Ikhnaton there was only one answer: He had committed himself to the rule of Aton throughout the world, a rule of peace. The people of the world would have to be educated for peace. They must learn how to live like the citizens of Akhetaton. In his desire to make Atonism world-wide, the king had in fact built an Aton-city in each of the three main divisions of the Egyptian Empire. In addition to Akhetaton, he founded holy cities in Asia and Nubia. The Nubian city was located at the Third Cataract on the east bank of the Nile (modern Dulgo) and was called "Gem-Aton." The Asiatic city was built in Syria but its exact location is unknown. Here in his own city of the sun the great dream had come true. He had proved that a community could exist without bloodshed, hatred, poverty and crime. Here the common people had their own homes and jobs. Slaves were not oppressed. Artists and farmers, scribes and tomb builders alike were happy in their work. While the Nile was in flood, the construction crews worked on buildings and roads. When the river receded, the grain was planted and the soil cultivated. Aton was good to all. His city was an example of how life should be lived. "It is not Aton's will," the king may have said, "that we go to foreign lands to fight. It may be that we shall lose our provincial possessions. That is preferable to violation of God's law."

With the populace deprived of the old deities and of the moral sanctions they provided, general disruption of the social order — with its ensuing moral chaos — was probably inevitable. Attempts to incorporate Atonism into the traditional religion of the people were no doubt confusing and ineffectual. Thus, the revolutionary theism of the pacifistic king remained confined to the court and loyal nobles of Akhetaton.

The real opposition to Atonism came not from the people, but from the Amon priests at Thebes, where the great empty temples served as a constant reminder of their disgrace at the hands of the heretic king, and from the military officers, whose memory of former conquests aroused their indignation. It is difficult, therefore, to understand why rebellion had not already broken out in Thebes.

Added to the danger of imminent revolt in the former

capital was the more ominous situation at Akhetaton itself. The last few years of the reign were ill-fated ones for the royal house. Ikhnaton was afflicted with congenital abnormalities and had always been in poor health. Now he felt his grasp on life slipping away as one tragedy after another plunged him deeper and deeper into a state of melancholy. Nefertiti had given birth to a seventh daughter, and it became a matter of grave concern at the court that there was no male heir to the throne. At the suggestion of the queen mother and Ay, Meritaton, the oldest daughter, was married to Smenkhkara, a young nobleman, who promptly took up residence at the court and began his training for the coregency. As time went on, the king relied more and more on his son-in-law, finally naming him as his successor.

Shortly after this decree, the palace announced the death of Tiy. True to his vow never to leave his capital, Ikhnaton remained in Amarna while Ay and Smenkhkara took the body of the queen to Thebes where she was buried near the tombs of Yuaa and Tuaa, her father and mother. The fact that she was permitted burial in Thebes is positive proof that she had not been wholeheartedly in favor of her son's religious revolution and had, moreover, stayed in Thebes most of the time.

Tiy's death was followed immediately by that of Maketaton, the second oldest daughter, who had been a victim of the same malady that afflicted the king. She was buried in a rock tomb on the outskirts of the city. Ikhnaton did not believe in death, either for Aton or for himself. But now death had struck at Amarna. The king had very reluctantly supervised the construction of his tomb and those of the nobles. But there were no embalmers in Akhetaton. He ordered undertakers to come from Thebes, but they refused to appear unless the Amon funerary ritual of seventy days was observed. This was a bitter pill for the king to swallow, but he finally agreed. The embalming process was duly carried out. However, Maketaton's funeral was unaccompanied by the customary ritualistic dancing and wailing. The long, hot journey to the tomb was made in silence. The body was laid in one of the halls of the royal tomb. Nefertiti placed upon the coffin a small wreath of flowers. The king waited until the lid of the coffin was in place and the doors of the chamber and tomb were sealed, then sadly returned to the city.

This series of events could only be viewed as the curse of Amon; tragedy at home was added to treachery abroad. Tributes from Asia, which had formerly poured into the City of the Horizon, now ceased. Workmen were unpaid and storehouses were empty. The Nile itself, source of all life, had failed for two years to overflow, and famine threatened the land. Tablets containing tragic news continued to arrive by weary messengers from the north. The faithful general, Horemheb, informed the king repeatedly of the treachery of Aziru, the Amorite, and pleaded for action before it was too late. The king listened in sadness, restrained from retaliation and violence by loyalty to Aton. Instead, he continued to preside at the festivals of Aton and to appear at all formal occasions, accompanied by Smenkhkara, Meritaton, and Nefertiti.

But as time went on chaos in the government, the empty treasuries, anger among the priests of Amon at Thebes, the discontent of the army officers and soldiers — restive under their forced idleness — all combined with Ikhnaton's failing health to overwhelm his spirits and plunge him into the depths of despair. He could no longer stand against the weight of impending disaster. Many of the duties connected with the government and the temple fell to Nefertiti. It was only her companionship that kept the ailing and sorrowing monarch alive during those trying days. But even her tender care could not protect Ikhnaton from the disease which had caused his father's premature death. He fell seriously ill and a pall of silence hung over the city and the court. The royal physician looked helplessly at the deformed and bloated body. Ikhnaton died in 1358 B.C. during the seventeenth year of his reign.

He was buried in the rock tomb which he had prepared for himself in the hills where Maketaton rested. The tomb was situated in a small *wadi* midway between the northern and southern groups of tombs. A descent of twelve steps led to a vestibule or entrance platform from which a second flight of steps led to the burial chamber. The walls of the tomb had been decorated with paintings showing scenes from the king's life. One relief shows the royal family at worship. In the nearby tomb chamber of Maketaton the walls were covered with scenes of the funeral of the princess. Pieces of the king's sarcophagus have been found in the tomb, but the canopic jars, which were made to hold the vital organs, show no sign of having been used. The royal artists had designed a beautiful coffin with a carved head covered by gold foil. The mummy was wrapped in sheets of pure gold and a gold necklace was placed around his neck by Nefertiti. An inscription on gold foil was placed at his feet. It was a prayer composed by the king himself who requested that it be buried with him.

In the restoration period, Ikhnaton's body was taken from Akhetaton and placed in his mother's tomb in the Valley of the Kings. Still later, this tomb was reopened; the name of Ikhnaton was erased wherever found, and the queen's body was removed to the tomb of her husband, Amenhotep III. The tomb in which she had lain, now considered by the fanatical Amon priests to be polluted by the presence of the "criminal of Akhetaton," was partially destroyed and then sealed again.

When Ikhnaton's mummy was discovered in 1907, it was taken to the Cairo Museum where it lay in a packing box for several years until rescued by James H. Breasted. During the restitution of the mummy, the king's prayer to Aton, which had lain at his feet, was found and, when translated, read: "I shall breathe the sweet breath which comes forth from thy mouth. I shall behold thy beauty every day. It is my desire that I may hear thy sweet voice, even the north wind, that my limbs may be quickened with life through love of thee. Give me thy hands, holding thy spirit, that I may receive it, and may live by it. Call thou upon my name throughout eternity, and it shall never fail." No more poignant lines are found in all history.

Smenkhkara's reign was brief and uneventful. Shortly after Ikhnaton's death, the new king, accompanied by Meritaton, went on an expedition to Memphis to see what measures could be taken to relieve the starving people. During the journey, Smenkhkara was fatally stricken with a disease of the marsh lands and was soon followed by his young bride, who had refused to leave his side.

Smenkhkara was succeeded by Tutankhaton, whom Horemheb had brought from Thebes in the early years of Ikhnaton's reign. He had seen to the boy's court tutelage and to his marriage to Ikhnaton's third daughter, Ankhsenpaton. Tutankhaton began his reign as a loyal follower of his father-in-law in the worship of Aton and remained so for some time, long enough at least to have his artists build him a beautiful golden throne, the back of which pictures himself and his wife seated under the Aton disc with the human-handed rays. It is remarkable that Tutankhaton was able to continue residence at Amarna as long as he did, in the face of the growing opposition — a fact which may have been due to the domination of Nefertiti over the boy, for with her there was no surrender to the forces of reaction.

By the second year of his reign, the new king found the changing climate of opinion too strong to resist. Both he and his queen, forced to espouse the worship of Amon, changed their names to Tutankhamon and Ankhsenamon. Although undoubtedly under the influence of Nefertiti, Tutankhamon still relied mainly on Horemheb's judgment, for he owed his career to the general. Caught between the pressures of both, Tutankhamon finally decided to follow the advice of Horemheb and return to Thebes.

Preparations were made promptly for the transfer of the court. Public buildings were sealed, but most of the records of the Foreign Office were left behind because of the uncertainty of the future. The nobles left their homes intact under guard. Grass began to grow in the streets, sand began to accumulate and the sacred lake dried up.

The royal *dahabiyeh,* which had been little used since it carried the heretic king downstream from Thebes, now slowly left the palace quay and started its laborious journey upstream. The young couple abandoned the City of the Horizon with great misgivings, for both realized that they faced an uncertain and ominous future. Akhetaton, fading in the distance, now seemed to hold all that was precious to them. But as they rounded the first bend in the river, Tutankhamon turned his mind reluctantly toward the future. Their arrival at Thebes freed their thoughts momentarily from the past, as they beheld the temples of Karnak and Luxor. They were greeted at the quay by the Amon priests and drove to the palace accompanied by troops and court officials.

Tutankhamon soon found the priests of Amon and the reactionaries rapidly assuming their former prestige. It was

*Photograph by Harry Burton, The Metropolitan Museum of Art*

Throne of Tutankhamon, showing the king and his wife under the sun-disc. Wood overlaid with sheet gold. From Tutankhamon's tomb at Thebes, discovered by Howard Carter in 1922. The continuance of Atonism during the early part of Tutankhamon's reign is illustrated in the decoration of this throne. Not only does the exquisite panel of colored inlay on the back of the throne show the king and queen overshadowed by Aton, but whereever the king's cartouche appears in inlay, it bears the original title of Tutankhaton; whereas in the gold work, which could be more easily altered, it has been changed to Tutankhamon.

apparent that the young pharaoh would have to conform or run the risk of dethronement. With the court re-established in Thebes, there was little to prevent the full reinstatement of the priesthood, the restoration of all the ancient deities — especially Amon — and the prohibition of Atonism. This involved a tremendous program of rehabilitation, not only in Thebes but throughout Egypt. From this point on, Amonism remained supreme, and all religious and artistic creativity vanished. The name of Ikhnaton was erased from every inscription that could be found, and the only permissible reference to him was that of the "criminal of Akhetaton."

We have previously mentioned the removal of Ikhnaton's mummy from Amarna to Thebes, where it was placed in the tomb of his mother. This act was probably the last loyal gesture of Tutankhamon and his wife, for it is hardly likely that Ay or Horemheb would have risked the enmity of the now powerful priesthood and nobles and it is inconceivable that the priests of Amon did it. But the deed did not escape the notice of the priests, who later removed the body of Queen Tiy and then desecrated the tomb, erasing the name of the king wherever they could.

The natural deterioration of the now deserted Amarna was aided by the reactionary groups, which destroyed the Aton temples and salvaged the stone blocks for the construction of new temples in Karnak. It is interesting to note, incidentally, that Amarna would be a perfect archaeological site today if these stone blocks had not been carried by the tens of thousands to Karnak. The site chosen for Akhetaton had never been built upon previously and no subsequent settlement was ever made there. Many of the laborers who had been left behind turned into robbers, plundering the palaces and tombs. The glass and faience industries probably continued for a short time, but like all other activities in the capital, they were dependent upon the court and therefore soon collapsed. Likewise, workmen of all kinds, bereft of the means of their livelihood, abandoned their homes and moved to other places.

It did not take many years for the sands of the desert to cover the remains of the once resplendent "City of the Horizon." And so vanished the dream city of Ikhnaton, lonely bastion of prophetic idealism, temple of light in a world of darkness. It had been "a fatuous island of the blest in a sea of discontent," as Breasted once described it, an idea born in the mind of an individual who did not reckon with human inertia and the weight of tradition, but who had the courage to create a universal ideal, even though the world was not ready for it. Years later the re-established priests sang triumphantly to Amon:

> The sun of him (Ikhnaton) who knows thee
> not goes down, O Amon!
> The temple of him (Ikhnaton) who assailed
> thee is in darkness.

His temple was destroyed, but his sun would one day rise again.

Nefertiti remained in the City of the Horizon. The North Palace was somewhat isolated from the rest of the capital and, for a while, at least, did not suffer from the wrecking operations of the Theban workers or from the ravages of wind and sand. The queen derived enough revenue from the northern customs office to support herself and her court. She continued to rise at dawn and go to a small nearby temple to celebrate the sunrise, the daily rebirth of the sun disc. A few priests probably remained in the northern city and served her at the temple.

Excavations at Amarna point to the possibility that, after the fourteenth year of Ikhnaton's reign, Nefertiti lived

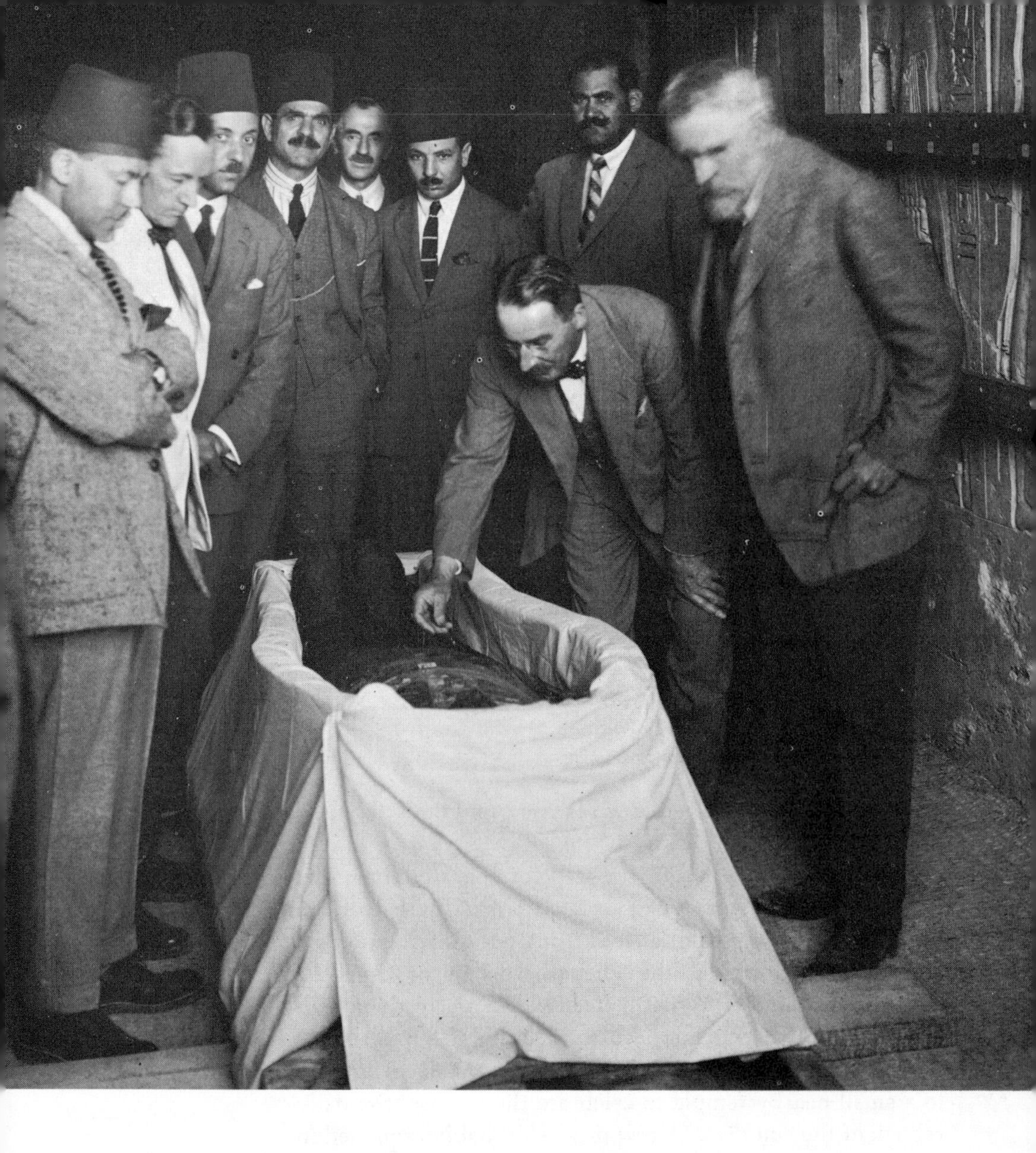

*Photograph by Harry Burton, The Metropolitan Museum of Art*

Howard Carter, the discoverer, and Dr. E. E. Derry, the anatomist, making the first incision into the mummy wrappings of the eighteen-year-old king, Tutankhamon.

in the northern city with Tutankhaton while the king lived in the main palace with Meritaton. This is mere conjecture, however, and is based on the assumption that there was a division in the court at the time with some favoring a return to Thebes and Amonism and others remaining loyal to the religion of Amarna. This theory has it that when Ikhnaton leaned toward surrendering the new faith, his queen, holding steadfast, removed to the northern palace, taking Tutankhaton with her. Ikhnaton, it is thought, made Smenkhkara coregent and sent him to Thebes on a mission of reconcilation. After Smenkhkara's death, the queen saw to the accession of Tutankhaton and his marriage to Ankhsenpaton. The documentary evidence is insufficient to support such a theory, but we can be certain that Nefertiti remained loyal to the Aton faith.

No evidence has ever been found regarding her fate. Nothing is known of the time or circumstances of her death or the whereabouts of her tomb. She probably survived her husband by only a few years. It is reasonable to believe that during the reigns of Smenkhkara and Tutankhaton and the latter's removal to Thebes, Nefertiti made no compromise with the ideals of the Aton reform. The remains at Amarna show that she ordered the royal artists to carve her name and that of her husband in all the buildings throughout her northern residence, which she called "The House of Aton."

The reign of Tutankhamon in Thebes lasted only nine years. During this time the restoration of Amonism and the obliteration of the Amarna heresy continued. Under Horemheb the army attempted to regain some of the Asiatic provinces, but nothing of military significance was accomplished. Tutankhamon's importance for us, however, lies not in his life, but in his death. His tomb, a relatively small one, was the only royal tomb ever discovered in Egypt that had not been opened and rifled by ancient tomb robbers. In 1922, Howard Carter and Lord Carnarvon found the funerary equipment of the young pharaoh intact and untouched after some thirty-three hundred years.

When Carter opened the sealed door of the tomb in the presence of the archaeologists and other dignitaries, an incredible and overpowering scene met their eyes. The burial chamber was lined with gold and blue faience inlay. The king lay within three coffins. On the outermost coffin, covering the head, was a mask made of gold, inlaid with lapis lazuli and semiprecious stones. This mask, evidently intended as a likeness of Tutankhamon, bore the *nemes* headdress with the uraeus and vulture symbols, representing Upper and Lower Egypt. Around the neck of the mask hung a beaded collar, and on its chin was a long Osirian beard. The second coffin was of solid gold. Guarding the sealed entrance to the burial chamber stood two identical gilded wooden statues of the king. One of the outstanding objects of the tomb was the wooden throne, overlaid with sheet gold, faience and gem inlay. On the back of the throne was a scene showing the king and queen and behind them the sun-disc with its human-handed rays. There were four chariots covered with gold, golden couches, alabaster vases and countless *shawabtis* (funerary statuettes), vessels, items of jewelry, furniture and statues. The flowers laid on the king's forehead by Ankhsenamon were still colorful amid the jewels and gold of the coffin.

From a journalistic standpoint, the discovery of the tomb of Tutankhamon was the greatest sustained news story of this century, excluding the two world wars. It had all the makings of an Agatha Christie novel and much more: years of searching for the lost mummy of the king, the accidental discovery of the tomb, golden treasures that staggered the imagination and the curse of Amon which

*Photograph by Harry Burton, The Metropolitan Museum of Art*

Head of Tutankhamon. The mummy, found by Howard Carter, is in the tomb at Thebes.

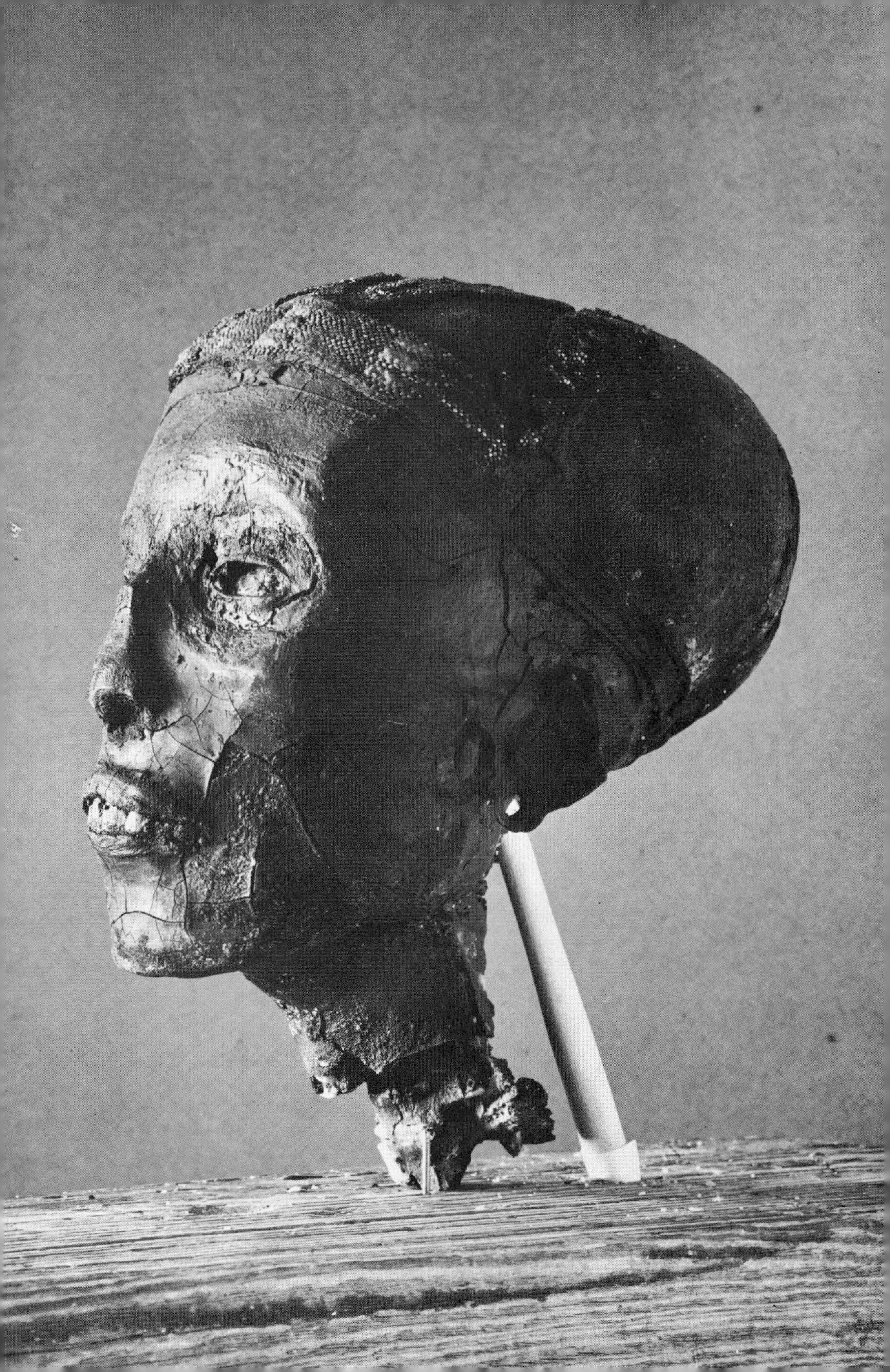

supposedly caused the strange deaths of twenty-four people connected with the excavation. Two factors contributed to the success of the mission and captured the interest of the world. One was the archaeological achievement itself which demanded a degree of technical perfection never before attained, and the other was the modern means of news coverage, photography and publicity.

One of the celebrated Boghaz-Keue tablets, written in Hittite cuneiform, indicates, at least to some experts, that Ankhsenamon, the widow of Tutankhamon, realizing her precarious position upon the death of her husband, wrote to Shubbiluliuma, the king of the Hittites, suggesting that she marry one of his sons. The king was suspicious and sent an extremely cautious reply. Ankhsenamon wrote again, assuring him of the fact that her husband was dead and that she had no son, and concluded: "So give me one of your sons, and he shall be my husband and king of Egypt." But the marriage that might have united the royal houses of Hatti and Egypt did not materialize. It seems that the Hittite king finally did send one of his sons, but he never reached Thebes! Ay and Horemheb saw to that. What really happened to Ankhsenamon is not known, but it is safe to assume that she was *persona non grata* in Thebes and probably was killed or exiled.

Tutankhamon was succeeded by Ay, the nobleman and priest who had been close to Ikhnaton at Amarna, but who, like Horemheb, had found it not too difficult to change his religious loyalties as he changed residence from Amarna to Thebes. At any rate, Ay saw no reason for continuing to uphold a lost cause. It was in his tomb at Amarna that the great Aton-hymn was inscribed and there can be no doubt of his loyalty to Ikhnaton while at Amarna. After moving to Thebes, Ay built a new tomb for himself in the Valley of the Kings. His unimportant reign lasted for about

*Photograph by Harry Burton, The Metropolitan Museum of Art*

Burial mask of Tutankhamon (1362–1352 B.C.), son-in-law of Ikhnaton. The mask, now in the Cairo Museum, is made of polished gold, inlaid with lapis lazuli, carnelian, alabaster and obsidian.

three years, and, with his death, the Eighteenth Dynasty came to a close. A period of anarchy followed in which robbers plundered the tombs of Thutmose IV and other prominent kings.

The throne was seized in 1349 B.C. by Horemheb, who restored order and inaugurated a new era in the history of Egypt. Horemheb's accession was the signal for the permanent abandonment of Amarna. The nobles had their homes dismantled and most of the wooden pillars were taken to Thebes. Many of the poorer people received permission to live in the homes of the wealthy. Throughout the Amarna period, Horemheb had been the close friend and adviser of Ikhnaton, but at the same time he had managed to keep in the good graces of the priesthood at Thebes. He was convinced that ultimately the salvation of Egypt lay in retaining a strong, aggressive army and a powerful Amon hierarchy. He had maintained a conciliatory attitude throughout the transitional reigns of Tutankhamon and Ay, but he knew that sooner or later the old order would have to be restored. Horemheb had no royal blood, but it was clear to the Theban priests that only in the hands of a military leader would Egypt have any future. His marriage to the princess Mutnezemt, sister of Nefertiti, was unnecessary as a means of unsurping the throne, but it did serve to strengthen his position from the standpoint of royal lineage. He proved to be exactly what Egypt needed for a period of restoration. He completed the demolition of Amarna by transporting all the remaining stone blocks to Thebes for the construction of new temples, effected a political and legal reform throughout the land and prepared the way for the more brilliant reign of Seti I, under whom Egypt regained a great deal of prestige as a world power although she never again attained the cultural achievements of the Eighteenth Dynasty.

The art style of Amarna fared somewhat better than did religion. Much of the religious symbolism of Ikhnaton survived. A good illustration of this is the now famous wooden throne of Tutankhamon, which depicts the king and queen in an informal pose before the sun disc with its human-handed rays. The wall paintings in the tombs of Tutankhamon and Ay definitely preserve the Amarna realism, but the most brilliant expression of this spirit was achieved in the Memphite tomb of Horemheb, which was probably built during the reign of Tutankhamon. The painting displays the same candid portraiture in the treatment of faces and human figures as the work of the Amarna artists. The continuing influence of Amarna, with its soft curved lines and freedom of movement, appears prominently in the Tutankhamon statue (usurped by Horemheb and now in Turin) and in the statue of Horemheb as a scribe (now in the Metropolitan Museum in New York) where the unconventional pose is far from royal. Politically, the reign of Horemheb marks the beginning of the Nineteenth Dynasty but artistically it belongs to the Eighteenth.

# Epilogue: The Success of Failure

Ikhnnaton might have been the founder of a lasting religious movement — the first monotheistic religion — but the times were not ripe. The man was ready for history but history was not ready for the man. The world was seething with unrest. The founding of a new religion requires a kind of situation that did not exist in the fourteenth century B.C. Furthermore, there were no great disciples of Atonism to carry it to the world. As for Egypt itself, it is unreasonable to expect that a country steeped in animistic polytheism for two thousand years would learn overnight to embrace an abstract monotheism. Also, a tolerance of the past and a conciliatory attitude toward the present — so necessary for the effective spread and continuation of any new movement — were both lacking in Ikhnaton. The revolution of Ikhnaton was too hurried and precipitous to last. It was a sweeping reform but premature. The stream of tradition was dammed up for a moment in history but the unstable construction of the Amarna ideal was suddenly broken down and drowned by the flood of tradition that flowed over it. And it might be added that the king's deliberate attempt to erase all mystery and official dignity from his person was not conducive to the maintenance of his authority and prestige, especially among the common people. He encouraged his artists in their exaggerated candor so that they had no hesitation in caricaturing him in all his public appearances. Atonism never became more than the religion of Amarna, and it died with its originator.

Ikhnaton, therefore, remains a prophet, the first prophet in history and, in some respects, one of the greatest. Like all later prophets of the first order, he failed, at least in the eyes of his contemporaries. But a prophet appeals to the ages rather than the age. Like the Hebrew prophets, he subordinated the political destiny of his country to a spiritual ideal, trusting to the survival of the ideal in spite of political downfall. In the Amarna revolution we can observe the power of an idea to hold sway in the face of tradition, environment and the desires of the people. In an age of militarism Ikhnaton was the first to teach the doctrine of peace. He was the first to preach the gospel of the simple life. Only an inspired prophet could oppose custom and tradition, and, by the force of his personality, found a new religion. In Egypt, as in the later Hebrew culture, the validity of an idea depended upon its claim to antiquity. Kings and wise men appealed to the sacred tradition to gain sanction for their writings. Ikhnaton appealed to no ancient legend or law, to no myths sanctified by time. His religion was of the eternal present, the evidences of which were open for all to see.

From our vantage point of three millennia we are able to appraise the greatness of Ikhnaton with true perspective and deep appreciation. Consider his unique situation in the history of religion. The lives of all other religious geniuses of antiquity are legendary, little more than unreliable traditions. There is, in fact, great doubt about the historicity of some of the founders of ancient religions. Their original teachings are not extant, but exist only in the manuscripts of a much later date — manuscripts that were the product of so much editing and changing over the centuries that we cannot be sure that later transcriptions are at all faithful to the original message. Both lives and teachings are obscured by ecclesiastical and theological accretions so that no one can be sure of the facts.

No such conditions obtain in the case of Ikhnaton. His original writings on the walls of the Amarna tombs can be read today just as when they were originally inscribed. No manuscripts, copies or conjectures are necessary here. The evidence of his career and home life is faithfully preserved in stone for all to see. The disclosures at Tell el-Amarna today after thirty-three hundred years, including the wall paintings, the numerous busts of the royal family, the death mask of Ikhnaton and the mummy itself, give to the life and teachings of the heretic king a ring of authenticity not discernible anywhere else in the history of religion.

Most prophets are an integral part of the flow of history; that is, they are dependent to some extent upon both antecedent and environmental influences. There has to be a fertilization of the soil before the flower of their genius blooms. They stand upon the shoulders of previous and less important precursors, any one of whom might have gone down in history as equally great had the times been right. The situation produces the great man but he in turn transcends the time and turns the world into a new channel. Such geniuses were original, to be sure, but not profoundly independent of their age. Such was the case of a Jesus, a Luther or a Newton. But Ikhnaton was a mutation, quite isolated from both historical background and contemporary influences, except for the existence of the sun cult of Ra and the use of the term Aton by his father. Herein lies his genius. In the evolution of religious ideas, societies, as a rule, undergo a gradual growth through primitive magic, the worship of local spirits, national deities, anthropomorphic gods and finally monotheism. With Ikhnaton, a direct leap was made over all this evolutionary process to a cosmic theism that is not unlike that of Spinoza or Wordsworth. Ikhnaton's religion was not simply the worship of the sun. It recognized the vast creative force of the sun and the spiritual being of which the sun was a symbol. He called this invisible force "Heat which is in Aton," thus representing God as a dynamic, vital reality, creator of the sun and all forms of life. Aton was the source of all energy, the primal power behind all things, a formless essence, an intelligence permeating the universe. In fact, Ikhnaton intuited — as did Wordsworth — that God is one "whose dwelling is the light of setting suns." This was man's first attempt to define God in intangible terms and idealistic qualities. Ikhnaton's god was both transcendent and immanent, original causation and continuous presence. Such a philosophical conception could mean nothing to a people whose gods were tangible and whose worship was prescribed in a specific formula. In fact, such a naturalistic, nonceremonial type of religion has unfortunately had difficulty in making headway in any age, so it is not surprising that Ikhnaton had no following. His was a voice crying in the wilderness, a harbinger of things to come. Thus, against the black night of Egyptian anthropomorphic religion this brilliant comet flashed for a moment, a prototype of the best modern theistic thought.

In the midst of the stilted, standardized living of our day and of social and religious conformity, the personality of this heretic of Amarna is a fresh breeze of originality and courage. In the casuistry and dishonesty of public life today, it shames us to contemplate the integrity and utter frankness of this lone individual. The example of his sincere family life is a rebuke to the decadence of contemporary culture. In a world of war he preached and practised the life of peace. Surrounded by superstition and ignorance, he pursued the life of reason. His was the success of failure, reminding all liberals today of the inertia of the status quo. But it also confirms the necessity of paying the price for one's reasoned convictions.

While the reform of Ikhnaton failed and was replaced by the powerful cult of Amonism, the idea of the fatherhood of God, the inner experience of God's presence and the love of natural beauty were deposited in the cultural soil of the world. True, the reform of Ikhnaton left little impression on the total civilization of Egypt; but if it was negligible in the history of Egypt, it looms large in the history of humanity. Seldom has a voice sung such praises that were worthy of God, the universal Providence and Father of all creatures. To have stood alone against tradition and to have given expression to these universal truths is Ikhnaton's claim to greatness. His pacifism caused the collapse of the Egyptian empire; but that was the price of his idealism, and it is perhaps doubtful, for that matter, that Egypt would have retained her supremacy anyway in the face of the successive periods of ascendancy of Babylonia, Persia and Greece.

Ikhnaton's importance in the final analysis is in the field of religion. His thinking is especially relevant for us today because he saw religion as a qualitative attitude toward the universe, an attitude that, in his case, at least, resulted in an ethical way of life. Popular religion today is just about what it always was: a quantitative, prescribed code based on the doctrine of penalties and rewards. Ikhnaton's distinction lies in his devotion to ends rather than means, universal principles rather than petty dogma, a total attitude toward life rather than a specific formula of sacramental works.

Too often religion is conceived as a segregated compartment, divorced from the so-called " secular " life. The segment of life called religion has little or nothing to do with the other phases of life. This religious-secular distinction is a false one, a construction in which religion is merely a nominal function. If religion, instead of being merely one innocuous division of life, can be experienced as the very core of existence, the central harmonizing factor, the determining influence, then all of life can be religious.

Religion has always been defined by its instrumentalities or means. These means — the Torah, the Mass, the Church, the Bible, the Sacraments, the Creeds, the Rituals — are purely incidental to the culture of any given individual. As such, they are important as helps to the good life. But more often than not these man-made instruments are regarded as ends in themselves, and religion becomes concerned with times and seasons, feasts and fasts, do's and don'ts, calendars, rites and taboos. Evidently, there is a vast difference, as John Dewey pointed out, between *having a religion* and *being religious*.

Religion consistently tends to reduce itself to a specific code. The prophet gives way to the priest, and the original spiritual ideal turns into a legalistic and ritualistic cult. By following a prescribed formula, the devotee is assured of salvation; but he must keep in line.

So it was with all primitive tribes. The medicine man decreed what the people should do and they conformed. They were told what to wear, when and how to plant or hunt, what to avoid eating, touching or saying. These tribal customs have survived in most modern cultures. Every religion has experienced this institutionalizing process, which seems necessary for the protection and propagation of the ideal, but which in turn kills the ideal. The cultus, with its tangible and visible apparatus, misses the very point of pure religion. It does not plumb the depths of the soul; it does not offer the challenge of the unattainable, for it prescribes a routine of duties which can be done and done easily.

There have been a few individuals in history who have seen religion as a dedication to ideal ends and ultimate principles, as a progressive realization of divine truth rather than as a closed system of revelation, as a high way of living rather than as an orthodox way of believing. One of these was Ikhnaton.

The criterion for prophetic genius is timelessness or contemporaneousness. Ikhnaton's religion of cosmic theism is more challenging and more imperative in the shrunken world of the space age than it was in the fourteenth century B.C., because the present demands such a world outlook for survival. Only a cosmic and universalistic faith can raise mankind above the particularisms of the cults which divide men into rival religious camps. Only a common faith in the fatherhood of God and its moral imperative can unite people on a supra-sectarian level. To stay below that level is to rest content with the shibboleths and intolerance of tribal religion.

The cosmic religion of Ikhnaton has much to say to a generation that lives between two worlds, the one dead and the other unable to be born, a generation that reaches for the moon but has not learned to live in a civilized manner on the earth. Indeed, with the advance of the space age and new knowledge about other worlds, one should expect some theological revision in the near future. The issue boils down to this: Is God the God of this planet only or is He a cosmic consciousness? Is He a tribal deity or a universal reality? Is He interested in revealing Himself only at a certain point in time at a certain place through a certain man; is He concerned only with Christian history? The theologians must enlarge their ideas of God, man and history if they take seriously the findings of comparative religion, the history of religions, the facts of history and human reason. The present age will force us to reappraise the theological pattern of the Christian church and to re-evaluate our place in the cosmos. Christian theology, ignoring the implications of the Copernican theory, continues to maintain that the earth is the focal center of creation and the sole object of God's concern. The heliocentric theory, for that matter, is no longer an adequate statement of our knowledge of the multiverse, in which the solar system is a mere speck of dust. Our ideology still includes the ancient Semitic myth of the origin of life and the fall of man. It may well be that the earth is not the only planet that sustains life. It is entirely possible that many solar systems have the same or similar conditions found on our earth. Can we therefore consider ourselves unique? Perhaps the recognition of the cosmic immensities will force us to outgrow our provincialism and suicidal national rivalries.

The fact is that we can no longer find God by clinging to a primitive cosmology or to an anthropomorphic deity who deliberately intervenes in the process of earthly history, or, more specifically, the history of one section of the earth. No longer can we hold to our theological views as a special and unique revelation when the same views are held in every other religion. We are struggling toward a world civilization and some day chauvinistic sectarianism will be as anachronistic as chauvinistic nationalism. The world is rapidly shrinking, and we can no longer rub shoulders with other cultures and still claim to have the final or only religion. We shall have to unite with others on a supra-sectarian plane — the plane of spiritual and moral values — rather than insist on our theological particularisms.

The prophet-king Ikhnaton was still a child of his age

and could not escape all the restrictions of the ancient world, but in his dream of universalism he was born for this time. The cosmic or naturalistic theism, suggested in his universal moral order of *maat*, appears today to be the most adequate philosophical formulation for the coming space age.

Ikhnaton's reign was the most interesting in Egyptian history, a period in which human values came first, a period in which at least one man lived " in truth." For the first time in history a king defied tradition, transcended convention and insisted that his people regard him as a man, not a god. And so he lived — as a man — in truth and simplicity among his people, a man with a sense of humor, sympathy and courage. When Ikhnaton died, his contemporaries called him the " criminal of Akhetaton." Today, some thirty-three hundred years later, he is recognized as a prophet and genius, " the first individual in history."

# Chronology

There are as many dating systems for Egyptian history as there are Egyptologists. Any one of them is at best approximate, especially concerning the dynasties preceding 1200 B.C. The following dates therefore are not to be regarded as precise. The dating of some reigns (Hatshepsut, Ikhnaton) depends upon whether or not the co-regency is included in the reign. The dynastic dates of the Old Kingdom are given, but the reigns of the individual kings are uncertain and are therefore omitted.

The arrangement of Egyptian history by dynasties derives from the lists of the priest Manetho who served under Ptolemy Philadelphus (285–247 B.C.). These lists have been preserved by Josephus (first century A.D.) and some early Christian historians. Some of the chronological lists used by Manetho are extant, one of which is the Turin Papyrus, written during the reign of Ramses II. Other lists appear on monuments at Sakkarah and Karnak. The Palermo Stone from the Fifth Dynasty contains valuable information about the early dynasties. In addition to the above records, chronological data have been ascertained from various monuments, tombs, royal annals and letters (such as the Amarna tablets). The following list of dates is an eclectic one, based partly on Kurt Lange, John A. Wilson, William S. Smith, and James H. Breasted.

## Old Kingdom

### (First Dynasty–Sixth Dynasty)

| | |
|---|---|
| Accession of Menes | 3400 (3500?) B.C. |
| First and Second Dynasties (Thinite) | 3400–2980 |
| Third Dynasty (Memphite) | 2980–2900 |
| Zoser | |
| Snefru | |
| Fourth Dynasty (Memphite) | 2900–2750 |
| Khufu or Cheops | |
| Khafre | |
| Menkure | |
| Fifth Dynasty (Memphite) | 2750–2625 |
| Sixth Dynasty (Memphite) | 2625–2475 |
| Pepi I | |
| Pepi II (reign of 90 years) | |
| Seventh and Eighth Dynasties (Memphite) | 2475–2445 |

## Middle Kingdom

### (Ninth Dynasty–Seventeenth Dynasty)

| | |
|---|---|
| Ninth and Tenth Dynasties (Heracleopolitan) | 2445–2160 |
| Eleventh Dynasty (Theban) | 2160–2000 |

| | |
|---|---|
| Nibheptre Mentuhotep IV | 2160–2000 |
| Twelfth Dynasty (Theban) | 2000–1788 |
| Amenemhet I | 2000–1970 |
| Sesostris I (or Senusert or Usertesen) | 1980–1935 |
| Amenemhet II | 1938–1903 |
| Sesostris II | 1906–1887 |
| Sesostris III | 1887–1849 |
| Amenemhet III | 1849–1801 |
| Thirteenth Dynasty (Theban) | 1788 |
| Fourteenth Dynasty (Xoite) | |
| Fifteenth and Sixteenth Dynasties | to |
| (Hyksos or " Shepherd Kings ") | |
| Seventeenth Dynasty (Theban) | 1580 |

## New Kingdom or New Empire

### (Eighteenth Dynasty–Twentieth Dynasty)

| | |
|---|---|
| Eighteenth Dynasty (Diospolite) | 1580–1305 |
| Ahmose I (or Ahmes) | 1580–1557 |
| Amenhotep I (or Amenophis) | 1557 |
| Thutmose I (or Thothmes) | to |
| Thutmose II | 1501 |
| Thutmose III and | 1501 |
| Queen Hatshepsut (or Hatasu) | to 1447 |
| Amenhotep II | 1447–1420 |
| Thutmose IV | 1420–1411 |
| Amenhotep III | 1411–1375 |
| Ikhnaton (or Amenhotep IV) | 1375–1358 |
| Smenkhkara | 1358 |
| Tutankhamon | |
| Ay | to |
| Horemheb | 1303 |
| Nineteenth Dynasty | 1305–1200 |
| Ramses I | 1303–1302 |
| Seti I | 1302–1290 |
| Ramses II | 1290–1224 |
| Mer-ne-Ptah | 1224–1214 |
| Syrian interregnum | 1202–1197 |
| Twentieth Dynasty | 1200–1090 |
| Set-nakht | 1197–1195 |
| Ramses III | 1195–1164 |
| Ramses IV | 1164–1157 |
| Ramses V | 1157–1153 |
| Ramses VI | 1153–1149 |
| Ramses VII | 1149–1142 |
| Ramses VIII | 1142–1138 |
| Ramses IX | 1138–1119 |
| Ramses X | 1119–1116 |
| Ramses XI | 1116–1085 |

| | |
|---|---|
| Twenty-first Dynasty | |
| (Tanite Dynasty; priest kings in Thebes) | |
| | 1085– 950 |
| Smendes | 1085 |
| Herihor (Thebes) | to 1054 |
| Psusennes I (Pasebkhanu) | 1054 |
| Paynozem (Thebes) | to 1009 |
| Amen-em-ipet | 1009–1000 |
| Sa-amen | 1000– 984 |
| Psusennes II (Pasebkhanu) | 984– 950 |
| Twenty-second Dynasty | |
| (Bubasite) Libyan kings | 950– 730 |
| Sheshonq I | 950– 929 |
| Osorkon I | 929– 893 |
| Takelot I | 893– 870 |
| Osorkon II | 870– 847 |
| Sheshonq II | 847 |
| Takelot II | 847– 823 |
| Sheshonq III | 823– 772 |
| Pami | 772– 767 |
| Sheshonq V | 767– 730 |
| Partly contemporaneous with Twenty-second Dynasty: | |
| Twenty-third Dynasty | 817 (?)–730 B.C. |
| Pedibast | 817– 763 |
| Sheshonq IV | 763– 757 |
| Osorkon III | 757– 748 |
| Takelot III | 748 |
| Rud-amen | to |
| Osorkon IV | 730 |
| Twenty-fourth Dynasty | 730– 715 |
| Tef-nekht | 730– 720 |
| Bocchoris (Bakenrenef) | 720– 715 |
| Partly contemporaneous with Twenty-third and Twenty-fourth Dynasties: | |
| Twenty-fifth Dynasty (Kushite: Ethiopian) | 751– 656 |
| Kashta | |
| Piankhy | 751– 716; Conquest |
| of Egypt: *circa* | 730 |
| Shabako | 716– 701 (?) |
| Shebitku | 701– 690 |
| Taharqa | 690– 664 |
| Tanwetamani | 664– 653 |
| Saite Period: 663 to 525 B.C. | |
| Twenty-sixth Dynasty | 663– 525 |
| Psamtik I (Wah-ib-ra) | 663– 609 |
| Necho (Nekau, Wehem-ib-ra) | 609– 594 |
| Psamtik II (Nefer-ib-ra) | 594– 588 |
| Apries (Haa-ib-ra) | 588– 568 |
| Amasis (Ahmes-sa-neith, Khnum-ib-ra) | 568– 525 |
| Psamtik III (Ankh-ka-en-ra) | 525 |

# Foreign Domination:

Persian Period: 525 to 332 B.C.

| | |
|---|---|
| Twenty-seventh Dynasty (First Persian Domination) | 525– 404 |
| Cambyses | 525– 522 |
| Darius I | 522– 485 |
| Xerxes | 485– 464 |
| Artaxerxes I | 464– 424 |
| Darius II | 424– 404 |
| Twenty-eighth Dynasty | 404– 398 |
| Amyrtaios | 404– 398 |
| Twenty-ninth Dynasty | 398– 378 |
| Nepheritis I (Naifaaurud) | 398– 392 |
| Akhoris (Haker) | 392– 380 |
| Psammouthis (Psamut) | 380– 379 |
| Nepheritis II (Naifaaurud) | 379– 378 |
| Thirtieth Dynasty | 378– 341 |
| Nectanebo I (Nekht-nebef) | 378– 360 |
| Teos | 361– 359 |
| Nectanebo II (Nekht-hor-heb) | 359– 341 |
| Thirty-first Dynasty (Second Persian Domination) | 341– 332 |
| Artaxerxes III (Ochos) | 341– 338 |
| Arses | 338– 335 |
| Darius III (Codoman) | 335– 330 |
| Ptolemaic Period | 332– 30 |
| Alexander the Great | 332– 323 |
| Ptolemy I (Soter) | 323– 283 |
| Ptolemy II (Philadelphus) | 285– 247 |
| Ptolemy III (Euergetes I) | 247– 221 |
| Ptolemy IV | 221– 203 |
| Ptolemy V (Epiphanes) | 203– 181 |
| Ptolemy VI (Philometor) | 181– 145 |
| Ptolemy VII (Euergetes II) | 170– 163, 145–116 |
| Ptolemy VIII (Soter II) | 116– 108, 88– 80 |
| Ptolemy IX (Alexander) | 108– 88 |
| Ptolemy X | 80 |
| Ptolemy XI (Auletes) | 80– 51 |
| Ptolemy XII | 51– 48 |
| Cleopatra VII | |
| Ptolemy XIII | 47– 44 |
| Cleopatra VII | |
| Cleopatra VII | 44 (?)– 30 |
| Ptolemy XIV (Caesarian) | |

# Index